MEETING JESUS

10 STORIES THAT CHANGE EVERYTHING

L. DAVID FAIRCHILD

LUCIDBOOKS

Meeting Jesus
10 Stories that Change Everything
Copyright © 2025 by L. David Fairchild

Published by Lucid Books in Houston, TX
www.LucidBooks.com

All rights reserved. No part of this publication may be reproduced, stored in a retrieval system, or transmitted in any form by any means, electronic, mechanical, photocopy, recording, or otherwise, without the prior permission of the publisher, except as provided for by USA copyright law.

Unless otherwise indicated, scripture quotations are taken from the ESV® Bible (The Holy Bible, English Standard Version®), copyright © 2001 by Crossway, a publishing ministry of Good News Publishers. Used by permission. All rights reserved.

ISBN: 978-1-63296-839-5 (Paperback)
ISBN: 978-1-63296-840-1 (Hardback)
eISBN: 978-1-63296-841-8

Special Sales: Most Lucid Books titles are available in special quantity discounts. Custom imprinting or excerpting can also be done to fit special needs. Contact Lucid Books at Info@LucidBooks.com

"David's exceptional clarity, faithful Bible exposition, and keen eye on the gospel help us encounter Jesus, story after story, chapter after chapter. This book will both inform and edify you!"

—**Jonathan K. Dodson**
founder of GCDiscipleship.com and author of many books including *Here in Spirit and Witness*.

"*Meeting Jesus* is a gripping call to meet Jesus face-to-face through the Gospels. My trusted friend, Pastor David Fairchild, vividly reveals Jesus's compassion, authority, and grace, challenging readers to shed self-reliance and embrace new life in Christ. More than stories, this book is a transformative journey into Jesus's love. A must-read for anyone craving a real encounter with the Savior."

—**Scott Thomas**
US Director of Great Commission Collective
Author of *The Gospel Shaped Leader* and co-author of *Gospel Coach*

"This book is what happens when a sharp theological mind and a deeply pastoral heart collide in the best possible way. I've had the privilege of watching David live out the truths in these pages with humility, boldness, and a deep love for Jesus and people. *Meeting Jesus* is an invitation to encounter the living Christ soaked in grace and grounded in Scripture. Whether you've been walking with Jesus for decades or are just starting to ask questions, this book will draw you closer to Him. Read it slowly. Wrestle with it honestly. And prepare to encounter Jesus in a way that just might change everything."

—Noel Jesse Heikkinen
Lead Pastor at Riverview Church and author of
Unchained and *Wretched Saints*

To Grace, the love of my life. Your love has taught me how to love Jesus more. And to our kids, Michael and Madison. You are my joy, my blessing, and daily reminder of God's goodness.

SPECIAL THANKS

A special thanks to Christ Community Church of Houston (www.c3houston.org) for the privilege of preaching the Word of God from which this book was born. Thank you for your support, your love, and your care. May the Lord bless His church through these pages.

TABLE OF CONTENTS

Foreword   xi

Introduction: Meeting Jesus   1

Chapter 1: Nicodemus – The Necessity of New Birth   5

Chapter 2: The Blind Man – Seeing vs. *Seeing*   27

Chapter 3: Faith That Amazes Jesus   49

Chapter 4: Faith And Friendship   73

Chapter 5: The One Thing You Won't Let Go   93

Chapter 6: The Scandalous Grace of Jesus   109

Chapter 7: The Thirst Only Jesus Can Quench   123

Chapter 8: The Resurrection and the Life   137

Chapter 9: The Widow and the Son   149

Chapter 10: Scandalous Grace – Jesus and the Sinful Woman   165

FOREWORD

As I read David Fairchild's delightful book, I met Jesus again. And when you meet Jesus, you are encountering the living, risen, and reigning Lord who is both tender and powerful, who understands our brokenness but has the power to bring healing. You do not remain the same. You are changed to become more fully human.

But as I read, something else happened as well. I was taken back to my own almost fifty-year long journey with the Bible from devouring it as a new Christian to preaching and teaching it to writing books on it. As I reflected on that journey, two things were in clear focus: the Scriptures are *personal,* and they are *powerful.* The Bible is personal: the living Christ comes to us in the words of Scripture. The Bible is powerful: the power of the living God by the Spirit works in the words of Scripture to liberate and renew us.

This is not always how I understood Scripture. As a new believer I loved the Bible and read it voraciously. I read it in a very personalized way as if God was teaching me directly. But I read it as doctrine or theology, what the Bible taught about many things that made up the Christian faith. I read it for "principles" to apply to my life. I especially read it as a book that would give me moral and ethical teaching, admirable virtues and desirable character traits, the way to live. I learned much and am deeply thankful for my immersion in the Scriptures in those early years.

But my way of reading the Bible was naïve and lacking. But even so, in spite of my inadequate understanding, Jesus met me in the Scriptures, and my life was changed.

My love for the Scriptures sent me off to seminary. I learned more how to read the Bible as an ancient document. I became conversant with the culture, the history, the literary, and the theological conventions of the day so I could hear what the original author was saying to the original audience back then. While I became much more adept at handling the Bible, I was still reading the Bible for theological ideas, for doctrine, for moral teaching. But again, I learned much because the Bible is always more powerful that our limited notions about it.

It wasn't until I planted a church, preached, and evangelized in the hard soil of a highly secularized urban setting in Canada that I would grow to see the Bible as far more than simply a book of religion that taught me true things about God and Jesus, sin and salvation, the Spirit and the Church. It was far more than a book on how to live uprightly. It did do all that, but it was much more. Daily I faced people who were a generation or two away from the Christian faith, who were enslaved to various idols of Canadian culture, not least the idols of consumerism, and they needed to meet Jesus in his resurrection power so they might be freed.

I struggled with many questions about this Bible I was called to preach and teach – what it was, what it was meant to do, how to read it properly, how it was different from other books. But I knew if my words were to be effective, I needed the firm conviction that, first, Jesus himself comes to us in the words of the Bible, and second, the Spirit's power changes, heals, and liberates us through the words of Scripture.

The reason I was sent back on this journey while reading this book is that it is clear David Fairchild understands this very well. As he unfolds these ten portions of Scripture, he knows that the purpose is to bring about an encounter between the living Jesus and his readers. And he also knows that such an encounter has the power to renew and transform our whole lives.

Once Jesus met a group of Jewish leaders who were also the biblical scholars of his day. They had memorized the Book of Moses and spent their lives studying, teaching, and writing about the Scriptures. They were almost certainly older men who lived a lifetime in the Scriptures. In comes this young man named Jesus, and he has the audacity to say to these seasoned leaders, "You have never heard God's voice" and "His Word does not dwell in you" and "You diligently study the Scriptures but you've missed the whole point" and "You love Moses but don't believe him" (John 5.37-47). I am sure these mature religious leaders were enraged with the impudence of this young man. And even more so when he says the reason their diligent study was to no avail was because these Scriptures testified *to him* and that Moses wrote *about him* (John 5.39-40, 46). The very words they studied should have led them to Jesus. And if they didn't, they were wasting their time!

The well-known 19th Danish philosopher Søren Kierkegaard similarly faced the biblical scholars of his day who spent their careers studying the Bible in the university. He didn't criticize them for their scholarly approach – he knew this was right and proper – but that this had caused them to miss the main thing – Jesus himself! He said, "If you are a scholar, remember that if you do not read God's Word in another way, it will turn out that after a lifetime of reading God's Word many hours every day, you nevertheless have never read – God's Word."

David Fairchild understands the importance of scholarship and reading the Bible as it comes to us – an ancient document. This is clear enough in the faithful way he handles the gospel texts. But he understands the main thing – all our scholarly learning should enable us to see and hear Jesus, to know his transforming power in our setting.

My understanding of this was largely the result of preaching and evangelizing people who desperately needed to know the renewing power of Jesus. It was during this time that Paul's words came home to me: the gospel is "the power of God that brings salvation" (Rom 1.16; 1 Cor 1.18, 2.4). These are not just words that give us new information and teaching; they do that but so much more! These are the very words of the living God through which the living and powerful Jesus comes to us to continue to save us from sin and idolatry.

It was also during this time of preaching and evangelizing that I came to understand that this was the way the great Reformers understood Scripture. Martin Luther said, "For Holy Scripture is the garment which our Lord Christ has put on and in which He lets Himself be seen and found." John Calvin uses the same metaphor. "This, then, is the true knowledge of Christ," he says, "if we receive him as he is offered by the Father: namely, clothed with his gospel." The person and power of risen Jesus comes to us clothed in the words of Scripture. I loved that image and still do! It enabled me to read and preach the Bible differently.

It was also during this time of preaching and evangelizing that I read the words of the great theologian Herman Bavinck. He says that Scripture is not only God-breathed but God-breathing (2 Timothy 3.16). Not only does the Holy Spirit breathe out the content of Scripture back then as ink on a page but continues to breathe through it today, making it come alive, leading people to Christ to be freed from bondage to all the powers that enslave. Eugene Peterson, a pastor and the author of the popular Message Bible translation, captures this. "We must beware," he said, "of turning the *living* Word into *ink* word." The words of Scripture must always be more than ink on a page, more than true ideas directed to the mind. They must become the very means by which the living Jesus comes to us in renewing power.

David Fairchild is a preacher and an evangelist. That is why I believe he understands well what Luther, Calvin, Bavinck, and Peterson are talking about. And it is clear in his book. It's why I met Jesus again while reading it and I think you will too! Come, encounter Jesus, and experience his transforming power.

Michael W. Goheen
Vancouver, B.C., Canada
Ascension Day 2025

INTRODUCTION:
MEETING JESUS

The Gospels are filled with stories of people who met Jesus—some by accident, others by desperation, and a few who didn't realize how much they needed Him until He showed up. These encounters aren't mere glimpses into history; they're windows into the heart of Jesus. They reveal how He engages people just like you and me and changes them forever.

Larry King, one of the most accomplished interviewers in history, was once asked whom he would most like to meet from the past. Without hesitation, he answered, "Jesus Christ." When pressed on why, King replied, "I would like to ask Him if He was indeed virgin-born. The answer to that would define history for me."

Here's a man who spent over 50 years interviewing the world's most powerful and influential people, conducting more than 60,000 interviews. Yet, he understood this profound truth: if Jesus is who the Bible says He is, it changes everything. Not just your personal story—it rewrites the history of the entire world. If Jesus really is the Son of God, born of a virgin, and came to bring redemption, then He's not just another historical figure. He's the figure who defines history itself.

And yet, for many of us, it's easy to miss Him. We can memorize verses about Jesus, learn doctrines concerning Jesus, and even build theological systems around Jesus, all while missing Jesus. We can study Him the way we study a historical figure or a philosophical idea—at arm's length. But Jesus isn't meant to be analyzed from a distance. He's meant to be encountered. That's why this book exists: to invite you to meet Him.

In this book we'll explore ten encounters with Jesus from the Gospels as Jesus meets people in their everyday lives. These aren't philosophical conversations about abstract ideas; they're real, flesh-and-blood interactions that show us how Jesus challenges and changes people in ways they never thought possible.

What's striking about these encounters is the diversity of the people He interacts with. He doesn't only engage the religiously inclined or the moral failures—He meets everyone. From the wealthy to the poor, the educated to the uneducated, the respected to the outcast, and the confident to the ashamed, Jesus seeks them all. In every encounter, He offers something extraordinary: Himself, showing that each person is of immense value to Him, while revealing the hidden need they have for Him.

As we walk through these ten transformative encounters, we'll hear Jesus tell Nicodemus, a morally fastidious religious leader, that being good isn't enough—he needs to be born again. We'll sit with a blind man on the roadside who couldn't see Jesus with his eyes but cried out to Him in faith and received both physical and spiritual sight. We'll watch Him marvel at the faith of a Roman centurion, a man of authority who understood what it means to trust an authority greater than himself.

We'll also watch as a group of friends tears a hole in a roof to bring their paralyzed friend to Jesus, only to hear Him address not just the man's physical need but his deeper spiritual need. We'll follow the rich young ruler, a man who thinks he has life figured out, only to be confronted with the one thing he can't let go of: his wealth.

We'll grieve with Mary and Martha, as Jesus steps into their pain with both tears and truth, showing that He truly is the resurrection and the life. We'll witness His tender compassion for a widow mourning her son as He restores what she thought was lost forever. And we'll stand under a sycamore tree with Zacchaeus, the despised tax collector, as Jesus calls him by name and invites Himself over for dinner and friendship.

We'll follow Jesus to a well in Samaria, where a woman burdened by shame finds living water. We'll also see a sinful woman anoint Jesus's feet, and learn what it means to be overwhelmed by the gift of forgiving grace.

Jesus still meets people today. He still confronts the proud and comforts the broken. He still exposes what's false and restores what's lost. And He still offers grace that transforms us from the inside out, showing that these encounters aren't just tales from the past but are powerful and life-changing today.

What's remarkable about these encounters is not only the diversity of the people but also the consistency of Jesus. He meets people where they are, but doesn't leave them there. To the proud, He offers a challenge. To the broken, He offers comfort. To the outcast, He offers belonging. And to everyone, He offers grace.

What's remarkable is that the same Jesus who walked the dusty roads of Galilee is alive and active today. He still seeks, still saves, and still transforms. The grace He extended to the people in these stories is the same grace He offers to us.

So, what would it be like to meet Jesus? The people in these stories found out, and their lives were never the same. My prayer is that you too meet Him in these pages. Not as a religious figure or an abstract idea, but as the living Savior who knows more about you than you know about yourself, who sees the real you in all your complexity and contradictions, and yet lovingly offers you something you truly need: Him.

Let's meet Him, because when you do, you won't be the same.

CHAPTER 1:
NICODEMUS – THE NECESSITY OF NEW BIRTH

Who Was Nicodemus?

The Bible is full of encounters with Jesus that leave people utterly transformed. Some are dramatic and unforgettable—lepers shouting for mercy, blind men regaining their sight, and tax collectors abandoning their greed to follow Him. Others, however, are quieter, almost understated, yet no less profound. The nighttime meeting between Jesus and Nicodemus falls into the latter category, but it is no less revolutionary.

Nicodemus wasn't the kind of person you'd expect to seek out Jesus. He wasn't sick or desperate. He wasn't marginalized or an outcast. He wasn't the kind of person society would label as "lost." By every standard of his day, Nicodemus had it all together. A Pharisee and a member of the Sanhedrin, the Jewish ruling council, he was a man of impeccable credentials. Respected, religious, and successful, Nicodemus was a shining example of moral and social achievement.

And yet, something was missing. Beneath the honors and accomplishments, a restlessness stirred in Nicodemus's heart. Perhaps it was curiosity—maybe he heard of the miracles Jesus performed and couldn't ignore the implications. Or perhaps it was something deeper: an unease with the limitations of the law to which he had dedicated his life. Despite his position and knowledge, Nicodemus couldn't shake the feeling that there was more to God than he understood.

This inner restlessness drove Nicodemus to Jesus under the cover of night. The timing is significant. John's Gospel frequently uses the imagery of light and darkness, and Nicodemus visits Jesus in literal darkness, a fitting picture of his spiritual state. It's also practical—Nicodemus likely wanted to avoid the prying eyes of his peers. Associating with Jesus, who was controversial among the religious elite, could jeopardize his reputation, career, and standing in the community.

Yet, despite the risks, Nicodemus comes. This single decision reveals more about him than his credentials ever could. It shows a man who is willing to seek truth, even when it challenges everything he built his life upon. It shows a man willing to step into the unknown, trusting that what he finds will be worth the risk.

In many ways, Nicodemus represents all of us. We may not share his title or social standing, but we all experience moments when the questions we suppress during the day become unavoidable at night. Who is Jesus? What does He want from me? What should I do with Him? Nicodemus's story reminds us that it's not enough to have the right answers or the right resume. Sooner or later, we must all come to Jesus with our questions and allow Him to speak to the deepest parts of who we are.

This nighttime conversation sets the tone for the rest of this book. Jesus doesn't meet us where *we* think we are; He meets us where we truly are. Nicodemus approached Jesus as a man who believed he was on solid ground, confident in his spiritual understanding. But Jesus saw past the exterior and went straight to the heart. Nicodemus didn't need affirmation for his efforts or reassurance about his standing; he needed something entirely different: rebirth.

This encounter shows that Jesus isn't interested in superficial conversations or polite religious discourse. He's interested in transformation. In Nicodemus's case, that transformation meant cutting through layers of self-reliance, religious performance, and intellectual pride to embrace a deeper truth: we cannot save ourselves. What we need isn't more effort or moral improvement—it's a new beginning, a total renewal of the heart and soul.

Nicodemus came in the dark, not fully understanding who Jesus was or what He offered. But by the end of their conversation, he would face a choice: to cling to what he had always known or to step into the light of what Jesus revealed. That same choice is before us today. Will we meet Jesus on His terms, or will we remain in the shadows?

The Opening Gambit

Nicodemus begins the conversation with a respectful, cautious tone: "Rabbi, we know that You are a teacher come from God, for no one can do these signs that You do unless God is with Him" (John 3:2). His words are carefully chosen, reflecting both curiosity and restraint. He calls Jesus "Rabbi," a term of honor and respect, and acknowledges the undeniable evidence of Jesus's miracles. But notice what Nicodemus doesn't say. He stops short of calling Jesus the Messiah or confessing personal faith. His opening is polite and safe, as if he's testing the waters, unsure of how Jesus will respond.

Perhaps Nicodemus hoped to establish common ground. As a Pharisee and a member of the Sanhedrin, he was accustomed to theological debates, where compliments often preceded serious discussions. Maybe he thought his acknowledgment of Jesus's divine authority would earn him a similar affirmation in return.

But Jesus doesn't engage in pleasantries. He doesn't thank Nicodemus for the compliment or return one of His own. Instead, He responds with a statement that cuts through the formalities and goes straight to the heart of the matter: "Truly, truly, I say to you, unless one is born again, he cannot see the kingdom of God" (John 3:3).

This response is as startling as it is direct. Nicodemus likely expected a conversation about theology, the law, or perhaps the meaning of Jesus's miracles. Instead, Jesus turns the spotlight onto Nicodemus's own heart and introduces a concept so radical that it shakes the very foundation of Nicodemus's worldview.

Nicodemus built his life on the belief that righteousness could be achieved through discipline, obedience, and meticulous religious observance. He devoted himself to the law, carefully following its commands and teaching others to do the same. In his mind, he was on the path to the kingdom of God. If anyone was qualified to see it, surely he was.

But Jesus's words dismantle this belief. To see the kingdom of God, Nicodemus doesn't need more effort, more knowledge, or more religious observance. He needs to be born again. This isn't just a call for self-improvement—it's a declaration that the transformation Nicodemus needs is so profound that it can only be described as a new birth.

This idea of being "born again" would have been as confusing as it was offensive to Nicodemus. Pharisees prided themselves on their lineage, their heritage as descendants of Abraham, and their meticulous adherence to the law. They believed they were already part of God's kingdom by virtue of their birth and behavior. Jesus's statement challenges all of that.

To be born again is to acknowledge that our first birth—our natural life, with all its privileges, accomplishments, and efforts—is insufficient to bring us into God's kingdom. It's an admission that no matter how righteous we may appear on the outside, we are spiritually dead on the inside and in desperate need of new life.

For Nicodemus, this was a paradigm shift. He came to Jesus expecting a conversation about signs and teachings, or perhaps even a theological debate. Instead, he is confronted with the reality of his own spiritual condition. Jesus isn't interested in discussing theories or doctrines; He is interested in Nicodemus's heart, and He knows that what Nicodemus needs isn't affirmation but transformation.

This moment is a turning point, not just for Nicodemus, but for all of us. It forces us to confront a hard truth: our best efforts, our moral achievements, and our religious practices cannot save us. Like Nicodemus, we may come to Jesus with a sense of our own sufficiency, thinking we just need a little guidance or encouragement. But Jesus meets us with the same radical truth: unless we are born again, we cannot see the kingdom of God.

Jesus's words strip away every illusion of self-reliance and demand that we start over—not by our own power, but through the work of the Spirit. It's not the message Nicodemus expected, but it's the one he needed. And it's the one we all need.

Born Again: What Does It Mean?

It's no wonder Nicodemus responded with confusion. "How can a man be born when he is old? Can he enter a second time into his mother's womb and be born?" (John 3:4). At first glance, his question seems almost absurd—was he really imagining a literal rebirth? But Nicodemus wasn't merely confused by the logistics; he was grappling with the implications of Jesus's words.

For a man who spent his entire life pursuing righteousness through effort and obedience, convinced that his spiritual pedigree placed him in good standing with God. Yet here was Jesus, telling him that none of that mattered. The path to God's kingdom wasn't through human effort or inherited privilege; it required something entirely different: new birth.

Jesus elaborated, "Truly, truly, I say to you, unless one is born of water and the Spirit, he cannot enter the kingdom of God. That which is born of the flesh is flesh, and that which is born of the Spirit is spirit" (John 3:5-6). These words are rich with meaning and point to a profound spiritual reality that Nicodemus, steeped in the Jewish Scriptures, should have recognized.

To be "born of water and the Spirit" is to undergo a complete renewal—a cleansing from sin and a transformation of the heart. This concept wasn't introduced by Jesus in a vacuum. It echoed God's promise in Ezekiel 36:25-27:

> *"I will sprinkle clean water on you, and you shall be clean from all your uncleannesses, and from all your idols I will cleanse you. And I will give you a new heart, and a new spirit I will put within you. And I will remove the heart of stone from your flesh and give you a heart of flesh. And I will put My Spirit within you, and cause you to walk in My statutes and be careful to obey My rules."*

Nicodemus would have known this passage well. It was a prophecy of the new covenant, a promise that God would do what humanity could not—cleanse His people from their sin and give them new hearts empowered by His Spirit. By referencing this imagery, Jesus was making it clear: entering God's kingdom wasn't about external rituals or moral achievements. It was about an internal transformation, a work of the Spirit that only God could accomplish.

Flesh and Spirit

Jesus continued, "That which is born of the flesh is flesh, and that which is born of the Spirit is spirit" (John 3:6). This statement draws a stark distinction between two realities. To be born of the flesh is to enter into the natural, human condition—a condition marked by sin, weakness, and separation from God.

No amount of effort or achievement can elevate what is born of the flesh to the level of the Spirit.

To be born of the Spirit is to receive new life—a life that isn't rooted in human effort but in God's grace. It's a work that begins with cleansing, removing the stain of sin, and continues with transformation, making us into new creations. This is what Jesus meant by being "born again." It's not about turning over a new leaf; it's about receiving an entirely new life.

The Radical Nature of Rebirth

For Nicodemus, this was a paradigm shift of the highest order. Jesus was dismantling his entire framework, revealing that salvation wasn't something Nicodemus could achieve; it was something God had to give.

This idea of spiritual rebirth isn't just a challenge for Nicodemus—it's a challenge for all of us. We live in a world that prizes self-reliance and achievement. We're taught to believe that we can earn our way to success, happiness, and even goodness. But Jesus's words confront us with the same humbling truth: we can't fix what's broken in us through our own efforts. We don't need improvement; we need resurrection.

Being born again means admitting that we can't save ourselves. It means letting go of our pride, self-sufficiency, and illusions of control. It means surrendering to the Spirit, trusting Him to cleanse us and give us a new heart.

This is why Jesus's words to Nicodemus are as relevant today as they were two thousand years ago. We may not be Pharisees, but we all have things we rely on to justify ourselves—our morality, our accomplishments, and our good intentions. But

Jesus reminds us that none of those things can bring us into God's kingdom. Only the Spirit can do that.

To be born again is to enter into a life that is entirely dependent on God. It's a life of grace, not effort; a life of transformation, not self-improvement. This life begins when we stop striving and start believing.

Nicodemus came to Jesus at night, filled with questions and uncertainties. He departed with a truth that would reshape his understanding of God and himself: what we need isn't better behavior or stronger effort—it's a new birth, a work of the Spirit that only God can do in us.

The Role of the Spirit
Jesus used a striking analogy to describe the work of the Holy Spirit: "The wind blows where it wishes, and you hear its sound, but you do not know where it comes from or where it goes. So it is with everyone who is born of the Spirit" (John 3:8). This imagery is rich in meaning, capturing both the mystery and the power of the Spirit's work.

The wind is unpredictable and uncontrollable. You can't see it, but you can see its effects. It bends trees, stirs up dust, and fills sails, making its presence undeniable. The Holy Spirit operates in much the same way. His work in a person's life is often invisible to the eye, but the transformation He brings is unmistakable.

For Nicodemus, this analogy was a radical shift in thinking. As a Pharisee, he was accustomed to structure, rules, and control. Faith, in his worldview, was something orderly and measurable—a series of obedient steps one could take to achieve righteousness. But Jesus revealed a truth that Nicodemus had never fully grasped: salvation isn't something we accomplish for God; it's something God accomplishes for us.

The Spirit moves sovereignly, bringing new life to those who are spiritually dead. Just as we can't summon the wind or dictate its direction, we can't command the Spirit or earn His work in our lives. This is a humbling truth, particularly for those of us who, like Nicodemus, are tempted to rely on our own efforts and achievements.

But it's also a liberating truth. If salvation depends on the Spirit and not on us, then our hope is secure. We don't have to strive to earn God's favor or wonder if we've done enough. The work of salvation—from conviction to regeneration to sanctification—is God's from beginning to end. Our role is not to control it but to receive it by faith.

The Sovereignty of the Spirit

The imagery of the wind also emphasizes the Spirit's sovereignty. The wind goes "where it wishes," and so does the Spirit. This reminds us that God's work in our lives is not something we can manipulate or engineer. The Spirit moves according to His own will and purposes, often in surprising ways.

This truth can be unsettling for those who like to feel in control. Nicodemus likely found it difficult to accept. To hear that salvation was entirely dependent on the Spirit's initiative would have been disorienting.

Yet this sovereignty of the Spirit is also a source of great comfort. It means that our salvation doesn't depend on our worthiness or performance. It's about God's grace, freely given to those He calls.

The Spirit's Transforming Power

The wind analogy also speaks to the Spirit's power. Just as the wind can reshape landscapes, the Spirit transforms lives. When He moves in a person's heart, the change is profound and unmistakable. He doesn't simply modify behavior or inspire good intentions; He brings new life, creating a complete spiritual renewal.

For Nicodemus, this was a foreign concept. As someone steeped in the law, he likely viewed spiritual transformation as visible external compliance—keeping commandments, offering sacrifices, and adhering to rituals. But Jesus pointed to something deeper: the Spirit changes us from the inside out, giving us a new heart and a new identity.

This is why Jesus described the new birth as being "of the Spirit." It's not about turning over a new leaf or trying harder to be good. It's about being made new by God's power, receiving a life that we could never produce on our own.

The Invitation to Trust

This teaching wasn't abstract or theoretical; it was deeply personal. By using the image of the wind, Jesus was inviting Nicodemus to let go of his reliance on rules and control and to trust in the Spirit's work. This invitation extends to us as well.

We live in a culture that values self-reliance and achievement. We're told that success depends on how hard we work and the extent of our accomplishments. However, the gospel turns this narrative on its head. It reveals that our greatest need—new life—can only be met by God's grace through the Spirit.

The role of the Spirit is deeply humbling and profoundly liberating. It reminds us that we can't save ourselves, but it also assures us that we don't have to. The same Spirit who raised Jesus from the dead is at work in us, drawing us to God, cleansing us from sin, and empowering us to live as His children.

Nicodemus came to Jesus seeking answers, and what he received was an invitation: to stop striving, stop relying on his own efforts, and trust in the sovereign, powerful, life-giving work of the Spirit. That same invitation is open to us today. Will we let go of control and allow the wind of the Spirit to transform us?

The Weight of Jesus's Words

Nicodemus, still grappling with the enormity of what Jesus was saying, found himself drawn into a story he would have known intimately: "As Moses lifted up the serpent in the wilderness, so must the Son of Man be lifted up, that whoever believes in Him may have eternal life" (John 3:14-15).

For a Jewish teacher, this reference to Numbers 21 would have struck a chord. In the wilderness, the Israelites were dying from venomous snake bites, a consequence of their rebellion against God. Desperate and helpless, they cried out for deliverance. God, in His mercy, instructed Moses to craft a bronze serpent and lift it on a pole. The solution was startlingly simple: those who looked at the serpent in faith were healed.

The parallel Jesus was drawing would not have been lost on Nicodemus. Just as the Israelites couldn't save themselves from the poison coursing through their veins, humanity cannot save itself from the poison of sin. Salvation comes not through effort or merit but through faith—through looking to the Son of Man, who would one day be "lifted up" on the cross for the sins of the world.

This imagery reframed everything Nicodemus thought he knew about salvation. It wasn't about climbing a ladder of righteousness or achieving spiritual perfection. It was about acknowledging our helplessness and looking to Jesus in faith as the only source of healing and life.

Then came the words that have echoed through the ages, resonating across cultures and generations: "For God so loved the world, that He gave His only Son, that whoever believes in Him should not perish but have eternal life" (John 3:16).

These words encapsulate the heart of the gospel. They reveal the depth of God's love—a love so vast and unmeasured that it encompasses not only Israel and the religious elite like Nicodemus but the entire world. It's a love that isn't earned or deserved; it's freely given, motivated by grace, and carried out through the ultimate sacrifice: the giving of God's only Son.

For Nicodemus, this must have been staggering. He likely understood God's love in more exclusive terms—reserved for the righteous, the obedient, the chosen. But here was Jesus proclaiming a love that transcended all boundaries, a love that reached not only to him but also to those he might have deemed unworthy: the sinners, the outcasts, the Gentiles.

But Jesus didn't stop with this declaration of love. He added a sobering warning: "Whoever believes in Him is not condemned, but whoever does not believe is condemned already, because he has not believed in the name of the only Son of God" (John 3:18).

The stakes could not have been higher. Without the new birth, without belief in the Son of God, we remain under condemnation—separated from God by the sin that infects every human heart. Jesus wasn't offering a neutral proposition; He was confronting Nicodemus and all of us with a choice that carries eternal consequences.

For Nicodemus, these words posed a direct challenge to everything he had built his life on. He relied on his adherence to the law, his status, and his accomplishments to stand righteous before God. But Jesus was making it clear: righteousness is not something we achieve; it is something we receive. And it comes only through faith in Him.

The mention of being "lifted up" would later take on even greater significance as Nicodemus witnessed Jesus's crucifixion. The image of the bronze serpent on a pole, bringing life to those who looked at it, would be fulfilled in Jesus, who was lifted up on the cross to bring eternal life to all who looked to Him in faith.

Nicodemus came to Jesus in the dark, seeking answers. What he received was an invitation— a call to step into the light of God's love, to leave behind the striving and self-reliance that had defined his life, and to embrace the gift of grace that could never be earned.

The weight of Jesus's words that night wasn't just for Nicodemus; it's for us, too. In a world where we are constantly told to work harder, do better, and prove ourselves, the message of John 3:16 cuts through the noise with stunning simplicity: God loves. God gives. We believe. We live.

But like Nicodemus, we must wrestle with the cost of that belief. It requires us to lay down our pride, acknowledge our need, and trust not in what we can do but in what Jesus has already done. The question remains: will we look to Him? Will we trust that His love, His sacrifice, and His grace are enough?

Light and Darkness

Jesus described the human condition with piercing clarity: "And this is the judgment: the light has come into the world, and people loved the darkness rather than the light because their works were evil" (John 3:19). These words cut to the core of our spiritual reality. They weren't just a commentary on Nicodemus—they're a commentary on all of us. Jesus wasn't merely describing those who openly reject God; He was unveiling the hidden inclinations of every human heart.

We don't just stumble in the dark by accident—we cling to it. The darkness feels safe because it conceals. It hides the parts of us we don't want anyone, including God, to see. Even when the light of Christ shines right in front of us, exposing our sin and offering a way out, we resist. Why? Because coming into the light requires us to face uncomfortable truths about ourselves.

Jesus continues, "For everyone who does wicked things hates the light and does not come to the light, lest his works should be exposed" (John 3:20). It's a hard truth to hear: we avoid the light because we fear exposure. We fear being fully known. The very idea of standing before God, vulnerable and without pretense, terrifies us. So we stay in the shadows, clinging to the illusion of control and the false security of our own righteousness.

Nicodemus, who approached Jesus under the cover of night, understood this tension. To step into the light would mean acknowledging he couldn't save himself. It would mean laying down his pride, his status, and his carefully constructed identity to receive a salvation he could neither earn nor control.

But Jesus doesn't leave the story there. He offers a way forward: "But whoever does what is true comes to the light, so that it may be clearly seen that his works have been carried out in God" (John 3:21). This is the invitation—to step out of the shadows and into the light, to stop hiding, stop striving, and let God do the work that only He can do.

The Choice Before Us

Jesus's contrast is stark: darkness or light, hiding or exposure, self-reliance, or surrender. The choice is ours. Will we continue to cling to the darkness, where our sins remain hidden but our souls remain enslaved? Or will we step into the light, trusting that the grace of God is greater than the weight of our guilt?

Jesus's words make it clear: stepping into the light isn't about proving ourselves or achieving some standard of goodness. It's about allowing God to work in us and through us. "Whoever does what is true comes to the light" (John 3:21). This isn't a call to perfection; it's a call to authenticity. It's about living in a way that reflects the work of God in our lives, not to earn His approval, but as a response to the approval He gives by grace.

Jesus was showing Nicodemus a different path—one that required him to abandon his self-reliance and embrace the transformative power of grace.

This same invitation extends to us. The light of Christ shines into our darkness, not to condemn us but to free us. It exposes our sin, yes, but it also reveals the grace that covers it. The question is, will we let go of the darkness and step into the light?

The Light of Christ

When Jesus speaks of Himself as the light, He isn't just offering Nicodemus theological insight; He's offering Himself. Jesus is the embodiment of truth, the source of life, and the one who breaks the power of darkness. Stepping into the light is stepping toward Him.

The light of Christ doesn't just illuminate—it heals. It reveals our need for grace while simultaneously offering it. It exposes our sin while covering it with mercy. It shows us who we really are and who we can become in Him.

Would Nicodemus step into the light, embracing the truth that only Jesus could give him what he had been striving for his entire life? This choice isn't just for Nicodemus; it's for all of us. The light has come into the world, and the invitation remains: step out of the darkness into the light and experience the life that only Christ can give.

What About Us?

Nicodemus' story doesn't end with this nighttime conversation. We catch glimpses of him later in John's Gospel, which reveal a man who seems to be grappling with the truths Jesus revealed. In John 7, Nicodemus tentatively defends Jesus before the Sanhedrin, asking his peers, "Does our law judge a man without first giving him a hearing and learning what he does?" (John 7:51). It's not a bold declaration of faith, but it's a step—a sign that the seeds Jesus planted are beginning to take root.

In John 19, after the crucifixion, we see Nicodemus again. This time, he helps Joseph of Arimathea prepare Jesus's body for burial. He brings a mixture of myrrh and aloes, weighing about seventy-five pounds—a lavish gift fit for a king. This act of devotion suggests that Nicodemus has come to see Jesus not just as a teacher or prophet, but as someone worthy of honor, even in death.

These glimpses of Nicodemus's journey remind us that transformation doesn't always happen all at once. For him, faith was a process, a series of steps from the shadows towards the light. And isn't that true for many of us? We might not experience a dramatic moment of conversion, but over time, as we encounter Jesus again and again, our hearts are changed.

But what about us? Where do we find ourselves in Nicodemus's story? Are we, like him, approaching Jesus with questions, unsure but curious? Or are we still attempting to earn God's favor through our own efforts, clinging to the illusion that moral performance is enough?

For some of us, the struggle might look different. Maybe we feel too far gone, too broken, too stained by our past to believe that God could truly love us. Maybe we've resigned ourselves to the idea that grace is for others but not for us.

Here's the truth Nicodemus discovered that night and throughout his journey: Jesus doesn't ask you to clean yourself up or figure it all out before coming to Him. He doesn't require you to meet a standard or achieve a certain level of righteousness. He simply says, *"Look to Me."*

Trust Him. Bring your questions, your doubts, your fears, and even your failures. Bring the parts of you that feel too messy to be redeemed. Jesus isn't intimidated by any of it. He sees you just as He saw Nicodemus, and He invites you to step into the light.

This is the beauty of the gospel: it doesn't rest on what you can do. It rests entirely on what Jesus has already done. He lived the perfect life you couldn't live, died the death you deserved to die, and rose again to give you new life. All He asks is that you trust Him, believe He is who He says He is, and that He can do what He promises—make you new.

So, what about us? Will we stay in the shadows, clinging to our self-reliance or our shame? Or will we step into the light, letting Jesus do what only He can? Nicodemus's story serves as a reminder that the journey to faith isn't always immediate, but every step toward Jesus is a step toward life.

The question now is not about Nicodemus—it's about you. What will you do with Jesus?

REFLECTION QUESTIONS

1. **What do you rely on for your sense of security and standing before God?** Nicodemus came to Jesus, confident in his religious knowledge and moral achievements, only to be told that he needed to be born again. What areas of your life might you be trusting in instead of trusting fully in God's grace?

2. **How does Jesus's call to be "born again" challenge your understanding of faith?** Being born again isn't about self-improvement but surrendering to the Spirit's transforming work. What does this truth reveal about the nature of salvation and your own need for spiritual renewal?

3. **In what ways do you cling to darkness rather than step into the light?** Jesus said people love darkness because it hides their sin. Are there areas in your life where you resist God's light and avoid the exposure that leads to healing and transformation?

4. **What does it mean to live as someone who has stepped into the light?** Jesus described those who come to the light as people whose lives clearly reflect God's work in them. How can you live in a way that points to the grace and power of God's Spirit in your life?

5. **How does this chapter deepen your understanding of God's grace?** Reflect on how Jesus's conversation with Nicodemus redefines salvation—not as something we earn, but as a gift we receive. How does this truth change the way you approach God and share His love with others?

Jesus's invitation to Nicodemus is the same invitation He extends to you: "You must be born again." It's an invitation to lay down your self-reliance and let God make you new. The question is simple yet profound: Will you trust Him? Will you look to the One who was lifted up for you, turn from your sin, and receive the gift of eternal life?

CHAPTER 2:
THE BLIND MAN – SEEING VS. *SEEING*

What would it mean to truly see Jesus? To experience a clarity so piercing that it redefines everything you thought you knew about life, yourself, and God? To move from confusion to understanding, from skepticism to trust, and from darkness to light? This is the journey of the blind man in John 9—a man who began his day in utter darkness but ended it in radiant worship, with his sight restored both physically and spiritually.

But this story is about far more than one man's blindness. It's a window into the condition we all share: spiritual blindness. The Bible describes humanity as "walking in darkness" (Isaiah 9:2), stumbling through life without perceiving God's truth or beauty. This blindness isn't just about ignorance; it's deeper than that. It's a willful refusal to see, a condition of the heart that clings to shadows even when light is breaking through. In so many ways, we are like this man before he met Jesus—blind to what matters most, unable to open our own eyes.

Yet the beauty of this story is that Jesus comes to the blind man. He initiates. He sees the man in his darkness and brings him into the light. As the man's physical sight is restored, something far greater begins to happen: his spiritual eyes are opened step by step. At first, he barely knows who Jesus is—"The man called Jesus" (John 9:11). But as the story unfolds, his understanding deepens. Each encounter with his neighbors, the Pharisees, and ultimately Jesus Himself draws him closer to the truth. By the end, he doesn't just see Jesus; he bows before Him in worship. It's a journey from blindness to belief, from confusion to clarity, and it's one we're all invited to take.

What's striking, though, is the irony woven through this story. The Pharisees, who are supposed to be the spiritual guides, are the ones who are truly blind. They possess knowledge but lack insight. They see the miracle yet miss the Miracle Worker. Their blindness isn't due to a lack of evidence; it's due to a lack of humility. How often does pride keep us in the dark, even when the light of Jesus is shining right in front of us? It's a sobering thought: sometimes, the people most confident in their sight are the blindest of all.

This story invites us to ask hard questions, but it does so with grace. Where are we blind? Where do we cling to darkness because stepping into the light feels too costly? But it also offers us incredible hope. Just as Jesus sought out the blind man and revealed Himself to him, He seeks us in our blindness. He asks us the same tender, probing question: "Do you believe in the Son of Man?" (John 9:35). And just like the blind man, we're invited to respond—not just with intellectual assent, but with worship.

This chapter is an invitation to clarity by stepping out of the shadows and into the light of Christ—not a harsh, condemning light, but a warm, illuminating one that reveals who we are and, more importantly, who He is. To truly see Jesus is to be transformed—not just in how we view Him, but in how we view everything. To see Him rightly is to worship Him joyfully. Will we open our eyes? Or will we, like the Pharisees, cling to the darkness we know? The blind man's journey reminds us that seeing isn't just a physical act—it's the courageous choice to let Jesus change how we see everything.

The Disciples' Blindness: A Theological Problem Instead of a Person

The story begins with Jesus and His disciples encountering a man who was blind from birth. The disciples notice him, but their reaction reveals a blindness of their own—not physical but spiritual. Instead of seeing a person in need, they see a theological problem to solve. "Rabbi, who sinned, this man or his parents, that he was born blind?" (John 9:2).

This question reflects a deeply ingrained assumption in their culture: suffering was directly tied to sin. If someone was born blind, there had to be an explanation. Perhaps his parents had committed some grave offense, or perhaps, in a mysterious way, he had sinned even before birth. The disciples weren't asking out of compassion—they were seeking an explanation, a theological framework to categorize his suffering. To them, the man wasn't primarily a person; he was a riddle to solve.

Imagine what it must have felt like for the man to overhear this question. His entire life had been shaped by these assumptions.

Every time he sat by the roadside, he likely felt the judgment of those passing by—their sidelong glances, the whispered accusations. He was not just blind; he was condemned. The disciples' question echoed the voices he had heard his whole life. It wasn't a question of care but of detached curiosity, reducing his suffering to a topic of debate.

But Jesus saw him differently. "It was not that this man sinned, or his parents," Jesus replied, "but that the works of God might be displayed in him" (John 9:3). In a single sentence, Jesus dismantled their assumptions about suffering and redirected their perspective. This man's blindness wasn't punishment; it was purpose. His life was not a theological dilemma but a living canvas for God's glory.

Jesus's response is both profound and unsettling. He doesn't offer a detailed explanation for the existence of suffering. Instead, He shifts the question entirely. The disciples were stuck in a "why" mindset: Why did this happen? Who is to blame? But Jesus invites them to ask a different question: What might God do through this? It's not about assigning fault but about anticipating redemption.

This reframing challenges us, too. How often do we view other's suffering as a problem to explain instead of a person to love? How often do we rush to assign blame—whether to others, to ourselves, or even to God—when we encounter pain? Jesus reminds us that suffering is not always about punishment; it is often an invitation to witness God's power and grace.

For the blind man, this moment marked the beginning of a story that would not only transform his life but also reveal the glory of God in a way no one could ignore. It is a call to shift from detached curiosity to compassionate engagement, from judgment to hope, and from asking "Why?" to asking, "How might God redeem this?"

Jesus Heals with Mud and a Command

Jesus could have healed the blind man with a word, but He didn't. Instead, He knelt down, spat on the ground, and made mud with His saliva. Then He spread the mud on the man's eyes and gave him an instruction: "Go, wash in the pool of Siloam" (John 9:6-7).

The method is unexpected—why mud? Why saliva? To modern readers, it might seem strange or even undignified, but every detail here is intentional. By using the dust of the earth, Jesus echoes the creation story in Genesis 2:7, where God formed humanity from the ground. This wasn't just a moment of healing; it was a moment of re-creation. Jesus was doing what only the Creator can do: restoring what is broken and making something new from the dust.

For the man, the command required both faith and action. Imagine the scene: blind, stumbling through the streets with mud covering his eyes, enduring the stares and whispers of curious onlookers. "What is he doing?" "Why is there mud on his face?" Yet he went. Perhaps he couldn't even fully explain why—only that he trusted the voice of the One who had touched him.

When he reached the pool of Siloam and washed, the impossible happened. Light flooded in. For the first time, he could see. Colors, shapes, faces—all the things he had only imagined—were suddenly vivid and real. What must that moment have felt like? Awe. Wonder. Joy. His entire world changed in an instant.

This moment wasn't just a miracle; it revealed who Jesus is. The man didn't earn his healing—he received it as a gift. His role was simply to trust and obey. While the healing of his physical sight was astonishing, it also served as a sign of something even greater: Jesus's mission to open spiritual eyes, leading people out of darkness into the light of life.

This story is also a picture of the gospel. Just as the blind man was powerless to heal himself, we are powerless to fix our spiritual blindness. Healing, restoration, and redemption come from Jesus alone. Yet, like the man, we're called to respond in faith—to trust His words and act on them, even when the path isn't clear, or the instructions seem unusual.

Through this seemingly simple act, Jesus shows us His heart. He is the Creator, who takes the dust of the earth and brings forth life. He is the Healer, who touches the broken and makes them whole. And He is the Savior, who calls us to trust Him, obey Him, and receive sight—both physical and spiritual—that only He can give.

The Neighbors' Response: Confusion and Doubt

When the man returned from the pool of Siloam, his neighbors and those who had seen him begging were stunned. "Is this not the man who used to sit and beg?" they asked, unable to reconcile the familiar figure they had known with the astonishing transformation before them. Some said, "It is he." Others countered, "No, but he is like him." The man, now able to see them for the first time, insisted, "I am the man" (John 9:8-9).

Their confusion is both understandable and revealing. This man's identity had always been tied to his blindness. He was "the blind beggar," a fixture in their community, defined by his disability and dependence. To see him now, moving with confidence and clarity, was nearly too much for them to process. It wasn't just his vision that had changed—it was his entire demeanor. His transformation forced them to confront the reality that something extraordinary had taken place.

This reaction reflects a deeper truth about human nature: when Jesus transforms someone, the change is undeniable, even if it's difficult to comprehend. It disrupts categories, challenges assumptions, and often provokes disbelief. We are quick to define people by their past—by their failures, struggles, or limitations. But when Jesus intervenes, He redefines their future. The neighbors' confusion reminds us how unsettling yet undeniable the work of Jesus can be.

As the questions continued, the man gave a straightforward account of his healing. "The man called Jesus made mud and anointed my eyes and said to me, 'Go to Siloam and wash.' So I went and washed and received my sight" (John 9:11). There is no embellishment, no attempt to explain the mechanics of the miracle—just a simple testimony of obedience and transformation. At this point, the man doesn't know much about Jesus. He hasn't yet grasped who Jesus truly is. He refers to Him as "the man called Jesus," indicating only the barest awareness of His identity. Yet even this statement is an act of faith. The man is testifying to what he knows: that Jesus had touched him and changed his life in a way no one else could.

This moment invites us to consider the power of a simple testimony. The man didn't have a fully developed theology or all the answers, but he bore witness to what he had experienced. Sometimes, that's all we're called to do. Faith often begins not with a comprehensive understanding but with an honest acknowledgment of what Jesus has done in our lives.

The neighbors' response also foreshadows the growing tension in the story. While some were curious, others were skeptical. The man's transformation was undeniable, but not everyone was ready to accept it. This is often the case when Jesus works in someone's life. His transformative power disrupts the status quo, challenging those who would rather remain comfortable in their disbelief. Yet the man's insistence— "I am the man"—is a quiet defiance, a refusal to let doubt or confusion overshadow the miracle that had taken place.

In this brief yet profound exchange, we see the beginning of the man's journey of faith. Although his understanding of Jesus remains incomplete, he has already started to testify to the One who changed his life. His transformation reveals a truth that is both unsettling and hopeful: when Jesus intervenes, He does more than heal—He redefines who we are, often in ways that leave those around us astonished.

The Pharisees' Interrogation: Legalism Over Grace

The neighbors, uncertain what to make of the miracle, brought the man to the Pharisees. Surely, the religious leaders would know how to interpret this astonishing event. But instead of marveling at the restoration of a man born blind—a miracle that had no precedent in Israel's history—the Pharisees fixated on a technicality: the healing had taken place on the Sabbath. Their rigid interpretation of the Sabbath law forbade any "work," and in their minds, making mud and applying it to the man's eyes counted as a violation.

Rather than celebrating an act of compassion and divine power, the Pharisees turned the moment into a courtroom drama. They interrogated the man, demanding to know how he had received his sight. The man answered simply and truthfully: "He put mud on my eyes, and I washed, and I see" (John 9:15). His words were straightforward, but the Pharisees' response was anything but. They splintered into two camps: some dismissed Jesus outright as a sinner for breaking the Sabbath, while others wrestled with the undeniable evidence of the miracle, asking, "How can a man who is a sinner do such signs?" (John 9:16).

The debate revealed a profound tension in their hearts. On one hand, they clung to their legalistic framework, which couldn't accommodate the idea that God might work outside their rules. On the other hand, they couldn't ignore the evidence standing before them: a man who had been blind his entire life could now see. But instead of allowing the miracle to lead them to faith, they allowed their legalism to blind them further. Their rigid adherence to the letter of the law eclipsed the grace and power of God on display.

Frustrated by their inability to reach a consensus, they turned back to the man, hoping to catch him off guard. "What do you say about him, since he has opened your eyes?" they asked. The man's response was simple yet daring: "He is a prophet" (John 9:17).

This answer marked a significant shift in the man's understanding of Jesus. At first, he had referred to Him as "the man called Jesus," but now he recognized Jesus as someone with divine authority, a messenger of God. His faith was growing, step by step, as he reflected on what had happened to him. Each interaction pushed him closer to the truth, even as the Pharisees remained entrenched in their disbelief.

Unwilling to accept his testimony, the Pharisees doubled down. They refused to believe that the man had ever been blind. Surely, this was some kind of deception, a fraud orchestrated to discredit them or confuse the people. So they summoned the man's parents, hoping to disprove his story.

This moment reveals the stark contrast between the man's journey of faith and the Pharisees' descent into spiritual blindness. While the man was moving closer to recognizing Jesus for who He truly was, the Pharisees were retreating further into their legalism and pride. They couldn't deny the miracle, but they also couldn't reconcile it with their narrow view of God. For them, the Sabbath had become a rigid rule rather than the intended gift of rest and worship. Their obsession with rules blinded them to the greater reality: the Lord of the Sabbath was standing in their midst, offering grace and restoration.

The Pharisees' interrogation reminds us of the dangers of legalism. When we prioritize rules over relationships or rituals over mercy, we risk missing the very work of God in front of us. Jesus's healing of the blind man wasn't just a physical miracle—it was a revelation of who He is and what He came to do: to bring light into the darkness, even the darkness of self-righteousness. But for those unwilling to see, the light only exposes their blindness.

The Parents' Fear: Silence in the Face of Truth

The Pharisees, desperate to discredit the man's testimony, summoned his parents to verify his story. They confirmed the basics: yes, this was their son, and yes, he had been born blind. But when pressed to explain how he had regained his sight, they hesitated. "He is of age; ask him," they said, deflecting the question back to their son (John 9:21).

It's a puzzling response. Their son, blind from birth, had just experienced a life-altering miracle; yet they offered no celebration, no affirmation, and no defense of the one who had healed him. Instead, they distanced themselves from the situation entirely. Why? John provides the answer: "His parents said these things because they feared the Jews, for the Jews had already agreed that if anyone should confess Jesus to be Christ, he was to be put out of the synagogue" (John 9:22).

To be cast out of the synagogue was no small consequence. It wasn't merely about losing a place of worship—it meant being excommunicated from the community, severing ties with family, friends, and neighbors. In a culture where identity and survival were deeply tied to one's social network, this was devastating. It meant economic hardship, isolation, and public shame. The parents, caught between the undeniable truth of their son's healing and the fear of rejection, chose silence.

Their reaction is a sobering reminder of how fear can paralyze faith. Instead of celebrating God's work in their son's life, they allowed their fear to dominate their response. Their silence wasn't just a refusal to speak; it was a refusal to take a stand, to risk the cost of acknowledging the truth. They prioritized the security of their position over the joy of proclaiming what God had done.

This moment invites us to reflect on our own responses to fear. How often do we remain silent when we should speak up? How often do we downplay or ignore God's work in our lives because we're afraid of what others might think? The fear of rejection, ridicule, or loss can be powerful, often tempting us to compromise our faith or avoid the truth altogether. Like the man's parents, we may find ourselves valuing the approval of people more than the glory of God.

Yet their silence also stands in stark contrast to their son's courage. Where they chose self-preservation, he chose to testify. Where they were paralyzed by fear, he stepped forward with boldness, even at great personal risk. His willingness to speak about Jesus, despite the pressure from the Pharisees, reveals the growing strength of his faith—a faith that his parents, ironically, could have learned from.

The parents' fear reminds us that faith often requires risk. Following Jesus may cost us relationships, opportunities, or social standing. But the alternative—remaining silent in the face of truth—is a denial of the very work God has done in us. Their story challenges us to consider how fear might be silencing our faith and to ask whether we are willing to trust God with the consequences of speaking the truth.

In the end, their silence couldn't erase the miracle. Their son's transformation was undeniable, a living testimony to the power of Jesus. Yet their refusal to celebrate it serves as a warning: fear may protect us in the moment, but it also robs us of the joy and freedom that come from proclaiming what God has done. Faith, on the other hand, calls us to step into the light, trusting that the One who opens blind eyes can also sustain us in the face of rejection.

The Man's Bold Testimony

The Pharisees, unwilling to accept the man's story, summoned him again for further questioning. This time, their tone shifted from feigned curiosity to outright accusation. "Give glory to God," they demanded. "We know that this man is a sinner" (John 9:24). This wasn't an invitation to worship; it was a call to renounce Jesus and align with their judgment. They cornered the man, trying to intimidate him into submission.

But the man refused to yield. His reply was clear, concise, and unforgettable: "Whether he is a sinner I do not know. One thing I do know, that though I was blind, now I see" (John 9:25).

This statement struck at the heart of their accusations. The man didn't claim to have all the answers about Jesus's identity or theological debates. He simply bore witness to what he knew—what Jesus had undeniably done for him. And that was enough. This is the essence of a powerful testimony: it doesn't rely on complex arguments or theological expertise, but on the undeniable evidence of a transformed life. The man's courage and clarity cut through the Pharisees' attempts to discredit him.

Frustrated, they pressed him again, asking, "What did he do to you? How did he open your eyes?" (John 9:26). At this point, the man's patience wore thin. His response was bold and even tinged with sarcasm: "I have told you already, and you would not listen. Why do you want to hear it again? Do you also want to become his disciples?" (John 9:27).

His words were a sharp rebuke, exposing their refusal to engage honestly with the truth. By suggesting they might want to follow Jesus themselves, he turned their interrogation back on them, forcing them to confront the question they were so desperate to avoid. The man's growing boldness revealed not only his courage but also the strength of his developing faith. He had nothing to lose—and everything to stand for.

His reply enraged the Pharisees. They resorted to insults, accusing him of arrogance and dismissing his testimony outright. "You are his disciple," they sneered, "but we are disciples of Moses. We know that God has spoken to Moses, but as for this man, we do not know where he comes from" (John 9:28-29). Their pride and self-righteousness blinded them to the very work of God occurring before them. They clung to their status as keepers of the law, refusing to entertain the possibility that Jesus might fulfill what Moses had written about.

But the man wouldn't back down. He answered with unshakable logic: "Why, this is an amazing thing! You do not know where he comes from, and yet he opened my eyes. We know that God does not listen to sinners, but if anyone is a worshiper of God and does his will, God listens to him. Never since the world began has it been heard that anyone opened the eyes of a man born blind. If this man were not from God, he could do nothing" (John 9:30-33).

This was no longer a man fumbling to explain his experience. His understanding of Jesus had deepened with each confrontation. He now recognized that Jesus was uniquely sent by God, empowered to do what no one else could. His testimony was grounded in both personal experience and sound reasoning, leaving the Pharisees no room to argue.

Unable to refute his words, the Pharisees lashed out in the only way they could: they expelled him from the synagogue. "You were born in utter sin, and would you teach us?" they shouted as they cast him out (John 9:34). Their rejection of the man symbolized their rejection of Jesus. Their pride, self-righteousness, and legalism kept them locked in spiritual blindness, unable to see the truth standing before them.

The man's testimony, however, serves as a powerful example of faith under fire. He had no formal education, no position of authority, and no deep understanding of theology. What he possessed was the courage to declare what he had experienced and the clarity to recognize Jesus's divine authority. His boldness cost him dearly—he was excommunicated from his community—but it also drew him closer to the One who had healed him.

This encounter reminds us that true faith isn't about having all the answers but about being willing to stand for the truth we know. The Pharisees' blindness serves as a cautionary tale of how pride and fear can block us from seeing God's work. In contrast, the man's testimony challenges us to speak boldly, even in the face of opposition, trusting that the truth of what Jesus has done in our lives is more powerful than any accusation or rejection.

Jesus Reveals Himself

After being cast out of the synagogue, the man was alone again. Rejected by the religious leaders and likely shunned by his community, he might have felt abandoned despite the miracle he had experienced. But Jesus sought him out. Jesus always seeks the marginalized, the rejected, and the weary. He finds those the world casts aside and draws them near. Approaching the man, Jesus asked a simple but profound question: "Do you believe in the Son of Man?" (John 9:35).

The man's response was humble and sincere: "And who is he, sir, that I may believe in him?" (John 9:36). Despite his boldness before the Pharisees, he still didn't fully understand who Jesus was. He had experienced Jesus's power and defended His integrity, but he hadn't yet grasped His identity. His question wasn't one of doubt but of eagerness. The man had already shown his willingness to believe, but now he wanted clarity—he wanted to know the One who had changed his life.

Jesus replied, "You have seen him, and it is he who is speaking to you" (John 9:37).

This moment is profound. The man who had been blind his entire life was now looking into the eyes of the Son of God. For the first time, his physical sight and spiritual sight aligned. The One who had healed him was not merely a prophet, a teacher, or a miracle worker—He was the Messiah, the Savior of the world. Jesus revealed Himself not as an abstract concept or a distant deity but as a personal Savior, standing face to face with the man He had restored.

The man's response was immediate and wholehearted: "Lord, I believe," he said, and he worshiped Him (John 9:38). This was more than intellectual assent—it was an act of complete surrender. In that moment, the man's journey of faith reached its culmination. He moved from seeing Jesus as "the man called Jesus" to "a prophet" to "a man sent from God," and finally to "Lord." His faith was no longer just about what Jesus had done for him but about who Jesus was. The only appropriate response was worship.

This encounter is the heart of the Gospel. Jesus doesn't merely improve our circumstances, solve our problems, or fix what's broken in our lives. He does something infinitely greater:

He opens our spiritual eyes to see Him for who He truly is—the Son of God, the Savior who invites us into a relationship of faith and worship. The man's story is a vivid picture of the transformation Jesus offers to all of us. He meets us in our blindness, opens our eyes, and invites us to respond in faith.

It's worth noting that this final moment wasn't just about the man recognizing Jesus—it was about Jesus seeking him out. Even after the miracle, Jesus wasn't finished with him. He didn't leave the man to fend for himself in the face of rejection and confusion. Instead, He pursued him, revealing His true identity and offering the man something far greater than physical sight: eternal life through faith in Him.

This story reminds us that faith is both a gift and a journey. The man's belief wasn't instant—it grew step by step as he encountered Jesus. In the same way, Jesus patiently leads us, opening our eyes little by little, until we see Him clearly. And when we do, our response can only echo the man's: "Lord, I believe," followed by a life of worship.

This is the essence of what it means to know Jesus. He doesn't just change what we see—He changes how we see everything. When we encounter Him, we're no longer defined by the labels others place on us, the fears that hold us back, or the sins that once enslaved us. Instead, we are defined by the One who gave us sight, called us to believe, and invited us into a relationship that leads to worship.

The Pharisees' Final Blindness

The story reaches its climax with a piercing and paradoxical statement from Jesus: "For judgment I came into this world, that those who do not see may see, and those who see may become blind" (John 9:39). With these words, Jesus lays bare the spiritual reality behind everything that has unfolded. The man born blind, who began the day in both physical and spiritual darkness, now sees with clarity—not just with his eyes but with his heart. Meanwhile, the Pharisees, who prided themselves on their spiritual sight, are exposed as blind.

Some Pharisees overheard Jesus and asked indignantly, "Are we also blind?" (John 9:40). Their question dripped with self-righteousness. Surely, they, the religious elite and guardians of God's law, were not among the blind. But Jesus's reply cut to the heart of their condition: "If you were blind, you would have no guilt; but now that you say, 'We see,' your guilt remains" (John 9:41).

The Pharisees' blindness was not due to a lack of evidence or ignorance. It was willful, born of pride and a refusal to let go of their control. They rejected Jesus not because His works were unclear but because His grace was incomprehensible. Their relationship with God was shaped by fear and works rather than love and grace, and, as a result, they could not fathom a God who would lavish mercy so freely. For all their knowledge of Scripture, they had missed the heart of God.

This blindness was reinforced by their reliance on religion as a system of control. For the Pharisees, the law was not just a guide to God's will—it was the currency by which they measured their worthiness and earned their place in God's favor. Their rigid adherence to the Sabbath regulations, even at the expense of compassion, revealed a deeper problem: they saw God as a taskmaster rather than as a Father and viewed His laws as a burden rather than as a gift. When Jesus healed the man born blind, they couldn't celebrate the miracle because it didn't fit within their system. Grace was too disruptive and too threatening.

This illustrates the danger of religion when it is driven by fear and works rather than love and grace. For all its potential for good—calling us to worship, moral living, and community—religion can also become an obstacle. It can blind us to the work of God if we reduce our relationship with Him to a checklist of behaviors or a set of rituals. Like the Pharisees, we can become so focused on maintaining our rules and traditions that we miss the beauty of God's grace breaking into our lives.

The Pharisees' response to Jesus shows how this blindness takes root. They couldn't comprehend that God could or would be so gracious. Acknowledging Jesus's work would mean admitting that their system was insufficient, that their pride was misplaced, and that their control was an illusion. Their blindness was not just a lack of sight—it was a refusal to see, a stubborn clinging to their own understanding of how God should operate.

This blindness is not unique to the Pharisees; it's a cautionary tale for us all. How often do we struggle to see God's work in our lives because it doesn't fit our expectations or because it threatens our sense of control? How often do we miss the wonder of His grace because we're too busy trying to earn His favor?

Jesus's statement— "those who do not see may see, and those who see may become blind"—is both a judgment and an invitation. It's a warning to those who rely on their own righteousness, but it also acts as a promise to those who recognize their need. The man born blind received his sight because he knew he was blind. The Pharisees remained in darkness because they claimed they could see.

The heart of the Gospel is that God's grace doesn't depend on our efforts or worthiness. It is freely given to those who admit their need, who stop striving to prove themselves and instead receive what Jesus offers. But for those who insist on earning their way to God, His grace will always be offensive—something to reject rather than rejoice in.

In the end, the Pharisees' blindness mirrored their rejection of Jesus. They were so bound by their fear of losing control, their pride in their status, and their dependence on works that they couldn't see the truth standing before them. Yet, the invitation remains: for all who recognize their blindness, Jesus offers sight. For all who admit their need, He offers grace. The question is whether we will humble ourselves to receive it—or remain blind, clinging to the illusion that we can see.

REFLECTION QUESTIONS

1. **Where do you see yourself in this story?** Are you like the blind man, experiencing God's transformative grace, or like the Pharisees, struggling to see His work because it doesn't fit your expectations or challenges your control?

2. **How might religion, rules, or routines blind you to the grace and work of God?** Are there areas where you've allowed fear, pride, or a reliance on your own efforts to overshadow the beauty of God's mercy and love?

3. **In what ways do you struggle to see or acknowledge God's work in your life or the lives of others?** What would it look like to move from doubt or resistance to faith and celebration?

4. **What is shaping your relationship with God—fear and works or love and grace?** How does your understanding of God's character influence the way you respond to His activity in your life?

5. **How can you cultivate spiritual sight?** What practical steps can you take to approach God with humility, admit areas of blindness, and open your heart to see Him for who He truly is?

CHAPTER 3:
FAITH THAT AMAZES JESUS

What kind of faith amazes Jesus? Imagine being someone whose trust in God is so extraordinary that even the Creator of the universe stops to marvel at it. In a world where faith often gets measured by outward expressions or bold declarations, the story of the centurion in Luke 7:1-10 offers a refreshing and challenging perspective. His faith wasn't loud or theatrical. It wasn't rooted in status, tradition, or personal worthiness. What made it remarkable was its simplicity, humility, and unshakable confidence in the authority of Jesus.

Throughout the Gospels, Jesus encounters a range of responses to His ministry—some believe wholeheartedly, others wrestle with doubt, and many reject Him outright. Yet, there are only two moments when Jesus is said to marvel. The first is in Mark 6:6, where He marvels at the unbelief of His own hometown, Nazareth—a place where familiarity with Jesus bred contempt and skepticism. The second is here in Luke 7, where He marvels at the extraordinary faith of a

Gentile—a Roman centurion whose understanding of Jesus surpassed that of many in Israel.

This juxtaposition is striking. In one instance, Jesus marvels at the absence of faith among those who should have known Him best. In the other, He marvels at the presence of faith in someone who, by all accounts, is an outsider to the promises of God. This contrast forces us to wrestle with a question: What kind of faith do we have? Is it like the faith of those in Nazareth—familiar with Jesus but indifferent to His power and authority? Or is it like the faith of the centurion—marked by humility, trust, and a deep awareness of who Jesus truly is?

The centurion's faith challenges us because it defies expectations. As a Roman soldier, he represented the occupying power oppressing Israel. He was a man of authority, accustomed to giving orders and being obeyed. And yet, when faced with a need beyond his control—the illness of his beloved servant—he didn't rely on his power, position, or influence. Instead, he turned to Jesus. His humility is evident in every detail of the story. He didn't even consider himself worthy to meet Jesus in person or to have Jesus enter his home. "But say the word, and let my servant be healed," he declared (Luke 7:7). This wasn't mere deference; it was profound faith in the authority of Jesus, a faith that recognized that Jesus's power was not bound by proximity or ritual.

The centurion's request revealed a deep understanding of who Jesus was. He grasped something many in Israel, including the religious leaders, had missed: Jesus possessed authority over sickness, distance, and all creation. He didn't trust in what Jesus might do but in who Jesus was, and this trust amazed Jesus.

This story invites us to reflect on our own faith. What made the centurion's faith so unique? Why was it so different from the unbelief of Nazareth or the shallow faith of the crowds who followed Jesus for miracles but didn't recognize His lordship? At its core, the centurion's faith was rooted in deep humility and a clear understanding of Jesus's authority. It wasn't about earning Jesus's favor or impressing Him with grand gestures—it was about acknowledging who Jesus is and trusting Him completely.

As we step into this chapter, we'll explore the centurion's faith and how it challenges us to rethink what it means to trust Jesus. Do we approach Him with humility, recognizing our unworthiness, or rely on our status, achievements, or self-righteousness? Do we believe in His authority over every area of our lives, or do we limit Him to certain expectations? The centurion's story is not just an example to admire—it's a call to cultivate a faith that amazes Jesus, a faith that rests entirely on His power, His grace, and His word.

A Crisis of Compassion

The story begins with a crisis—a moment of desperation and helplessness. The centurion, a Roman officer commanding a hundred soldiers, has a servant who is gravely ill and on the brink of death. In Roman society, servants were typically regarded as expendable property. Aristotle famously described slaves as "living tools," underscoring the dehumanizing view of servitude in the ancient world. A sick servant would normally elicit indifference or, at best, pragmatic concern from a master. But this centurion is different.

Luke tells us that this servant was "highly valued" by the centurion (Luke 7:2). The term suggests more than mere utility or function; it conveys affection, respect, and care. This wasn't just someone who worked for the centurion; this was someone he genuinely cared about, perhaps even loved as part of his household. In a world that often treated human life as disposable, the centurion's compassion shone as a remarkable countercultural virtue.

This compassion sets the centurion apart from the norms of his time and reveals something profound about his character. Here is a man of authority, a commander accustomed to giving orders and being obeyed without question, yet he doesn't see himself as superior. He doesn't allow his power or position to diminish his care for others. His willingness to go to great lengths for the well-being of his servant tells us something critical: humility and compassion are the soil in which true faith grows.

The centurion's compassion was not incidental—it was the catalyst that drove him toward Jesus. His care for his servant moved him to seek help from the only One who could offer it. This moment challenges us to consider the role compassion plays in our own faith. Too often, we view faith as an individual endeavor, disconnected from our relationships or concern for others. Yet here we see that faith often begins not in isolation but in the shared burdens of love and care. The centurion's concern for his servant created the space for him to turn to Jesus, not only for his own sake but for the sake of another.

This intersection of compassion and faith invites reflection. How often do we allow the needs of others to draw us closer to

God? Do we approach Him with intercession born out of love for others, or do we reserve our prayers for our own crises? The centurion reminds us that faith is not just a personal pursuit—it often grows in the context of community, where the needs of others drive us to seek God's intervention.

Moreover, the centurion's actions highlight the character of Jesus Himself. The compassion he shows for his servant mirrors the compassion of Christ, who consistently saw value in those society deemed unworthy. Just as the centurion's care transcended cultural norms, Jesus's love transcends all boundaries—ethnic, social, and even moral. When the centurion later demonstrates his extraordinary faith, it is no accident that it is rooted in a heart already shaped by compassion and humility.

This story also challenges us to examine our own hearts. Compassion and humility are not just precursors to faith; they are essential markers of a heart aligned with God's heart. True faith is not cold or detached—it is deeply invested in the well-being of others. The centurion's concern for his servant teaches us that our faith is often most vibrant when expressed through acts of love and service.

In the centurion's crisis, we see the beginnings of a faith that will amaze Jesus. It begins not with a spectacle, a demand, or even a personal need, but with a simple and profound compassion for another. His concern sets the stage for a powerful encounter with the One who embodies perfect compassion and perfect authority. In this, we are reminded that faith is not just about believing—it is about loving deeply, seeing others as God sees them, and allowing that love to lead us to Jesus.

A Helpless Commander

Despite his power and influence, the centurion finds himself utterly helpless in this situation. His resources, rank, and authority—qualities that likely served him well throughout his career—are powerless to save his beloved servant. This moment of helplessness is a turning point. It highlights a universal truth: no matter how capable or self-sufficient we may seem, there are circumstances in life that bring us to the end of ourselves. Often, it is precisely at this point—when we are forced to confront our own limitations—that faith begins to take root.

The centurion, accustomed to command and control, now faces a problem he cannot solve. Roman officers like him were trained to be disciplined, self-reliant, and decisive. In the face of challenges, they turned to their training, their comrades, or their gods. But none of these could offer him what he needed. The centurion's helplessness becomes fertile ground for faith. It is this crisis that drives him to Jesus—a Jewish teacher and healer whose reputation for miracles had likely reached even Roman ears. Hearing about Jesus was one thing; seeking Him was another. This moment reveals the first mark of great faith: dependence.

What makes the centurion's faith particularly remarkable is his willingness to step outside the boundaries of his cultural and religious context. As a Roman officer, he represented the occupying power in Israel, having no natural allegiance to the Jewish people, their customs, or their faith. In fact, Roman soldiers were often despised by the Jews for their role in enforcing imperial rule. Yet the centurion doesn't let these barriers stop him; he recognizes in Jesus an authority greater than his own—an authority that transcends nationality, religion, and rank.

This decision speaks volumes about the centurion's character. He could have sought help from the Roman gods or turned to his own community for solutions. Instead, he humbles himself and turns to Jesus. This humility and openness are striking. The centurion's faith is not bound by pride, prejudice, or the limitations of his upbringing. He is willing to look beyond his own preconceived notions and cultural loyalties to find truth where it truly resides—in Jesus.

This willingness to seek truth, even from unexpected sources, stands in stark contrast to the Pharisees. Unlike the centurion, the Pharisees had every opportunity to recognize Jesus's authority. They were steeped in Scripture, witnesses to His miracles, and experts in the law. Yet their pride and rigidity blinded them to the truth. They clung to their positions of power and their narrow interpretations of God's work, refusing to see what the centurion recognized so clearly. The centurion's openness challenges us to consider whether we are willing to lay aside our own pride and preconceived ideas in our pursuit of truth.

The centurion's helplessness is not a weakness—it is a strength. In recognizing his inability to save his servant, he demonstrates a key component of faith: the acknowledgment that we are not in control and that we need help beyond ourselves. This is a difficult posture to adopt, especially for those accustomed to leadership or self-reliance. Yet, it is precisely this dependence that opens the door for God to work.

This moment also challenges us. How often do we rely on our resources, status, or abilities instead of turning to Jesus? Do we, like the centurion, recognize our helplessness as an invitation to trust God more deeply? Or do we resist dependence, clinging to the illusion of control?

The centurion's story reminds us that faith often begins where our strength ends. It requires humility to admit that we can't fix our problems or save ourselves.

Additionally, it takes courage to look beyond our comfort zones, cultural expectations, and preconceived notions to seek the One who truly has authority. His willingness to approach Jesus, despite the barriers of culture and status, serves as a powerful example of what it means to have faith that amazes. In his helplessness, the centurion found the path to trust—and it was this trust that drew him to the only One who could truly help.

The Elders' Argument

The centurion's approach to Jesus is as surprising as it is revealing. Instead of leveraging his authority as a Roman officer to summon Jesus, he sends Jewish elders to plead on his behalf. This decision is significant. As a man of power, he could have demanded Jesus's presence, but he chose the path of humility and respect. The centurion acknowledges Jesus's Jewish identity and the cultural dynamics at play by asking the Jewish elders to intercede. It's a gesture that demonstrates his understanding of the situation and his deep regard for the customs and beliefs of those around him.

The Jewish elders respond enthusiastically, eager to advocate for the centurion. They approach Jesus and say, "He is worthy to have you do this for him, for he loves our nation, and he is the one who built us our synagogue" (Luke 7:4-5). Their words reveal much about the centurion's unusual relationship with the Jewish community. Typically, Roman officers were seen as oppressors—symbols of foreign rule and enforcers of imperial authority. Yet this centurion defied those stereotypes. Through his generosity and love for the Jewish people, he earned their respect and admiration. His funding of their synagogue was a tangible expression of that love, a gesture of goodwill that left a lasting impact.

From the elders' perspective, the centurion's good deeds made him deserving of Jesus's help. Their argument hinges on his worthiness, measured by his love for their nation and his acts of generosity. This appeal highlights a common human tendency to equate worthiness with actions. According to their logic, the centurion's contributions and kindness earned him the right to receive Jesus's help.

But this perspective, while well-meaning, reveals a profound misunderstanding of grace. The elders' argument reflects how human beings often think about favor and blessings. We're quick to assume that God's help must be earned through good behavior, moral uprightness, or acts of service. This transactional view of grace— "You do good, and God rewards you"—is deeply ingrained in human nature. Yet, it misses the very heart of the Gospel.

The centurion himself offers a striking contrast to the elders' view. Later in the story, he explicitly states, "I am not worthy to have you come under my roof" (Luke 7:6). Despite his accomplishments, influence, and generosity, the centurion doesn't consider himself deserving of Jesus's attention. He understands something the elders have missed: God's grace isn't given because we are worthy; it's given because we need it. This humility is the foundation of the centurion's faith and is one of the reasons it amazes Jesus.

This tension between human assessments of worthiness and the free gift of God's grace is a recurring theme throughout Scripture. While humans often judge based on merit, God operates on an entirely different basis. Grace is not earned; it is freely given. The centurion's story serves as a reminder that God's blessings are not rewards for good behavior but gifts for those who recognize their dependence on Him.

The elders' appeal also underscores the limits of human understanding regarding faith. They advocate for the centurion based on his deeds, but Jesus responds to something much deeper—his humility and trust. The elders see a man who is generous and admirable; Jesus sees a man who is helpless and dependent on Him. The centurion's willingness to send the elders, rather than assert his authority, is a demonstration of faith in itself. It shows that he is not relying on his position, reputation, or good works, but rather on Jesus alone.

This part of the story challenges us to examine our own assumptions about worthiness. Do we approach God like the elders, pointing to our accomplishments and expecting blessings in return? Or do we come like the centurion, aware of our unworthiness and trusting in God's grace alone? The elders' argument, though well-intentioned, reveals how easily we can slip into a works-based mindset, even when speaking about God's grace.

In the end, Jesus's response is not based on the centurion's generosity or the elders' argument—it's based on the centurion's faith. This underscores the radical nature of grace: it is not for the deserving but for the dependent. The centurion's humility and trust show us that true faith doesn't ask, "Am I worthy?" It declares, "I need You." And this kind of faith—a faith rooted in dependence and humility—amazes Jesus and opens the door for His power to work in our lives.

Unworthy but Bold

As Jesus sets out toward the centurion's house, the centurion sends another message that reveals the depth of his faith and humility: "Lord, do not trouble yourself, for I am not worthy to have you come under my roof. Therefore I did not presume to come to you. But say the word, and let my servant be healed" (Luke 7:6-7).

This response is extraordinary in every way. The centurion, a man of high rank and authority, views himself as unworthy in the presence of Jesus. Roman officers were accustomed to privilege, often demanding respect and submission simply by virtue of their position. Yet this centurion takes the opposite posture. Despite his status, accomplishments, and the respect he had earned from the Jewish elders, he sees himself as unworthy to even have Jesus enter his home. His humility is not born of self-pity or insecurity, but from a profound awareness of who Jesus is.

The Jewish elders had insisted that the centurion was "worthy" of Jesus's help because of his generosity and love for their nation. But the centurion himself understands something deeper: no one is truly worthy of God's grace. His humility is a cornerstone of his faith. He doesn't approach Jesus with entitlement or demands, as one might expect from a person in his position. Instead, he approaches with reverence, dependence, and an acute awareness of his own limitations. He understands that Jesus's power and authority are not bound by human worthiness, and he places his trust fully in Jesus's word.

This humility is paired with boldness. While the centurion acknowledges his unworthiness, he still asks Jesus to act. He doesn't shrink back in fear or doubt but demonstrates a confidence that amazes even Jesus. "Say the word, and let my servant be healed," he declares (Luke 7:7). In this simple statement, the centurion expresses a faith that is both humble and bold—a faith that recognizes Jesus's authority and trusts it completely. He believes that Jesus's word alone has the power to heal, even from a distance. This understanding of Jesus's authority surpasses that of many who have seen Jesus perform miracles firsthand.

The centurion's response also reveals his sensitivity to Jewish customs. As a Gentile, he likely knew that for Jesus, a Jewish teacher, to enter his home could make Him ceremonially unclean according to Jewish law. By asking Jesus not to come under his roof, the centurion demonstrates both cultural awareness and respect. This isn't a man trying to assert his own way; it's a man deeply attuned to the sensitivities of others, willing to adapt his request out of consideration for Jesus. His respect for Jewish customs and his reverence for Jesus's authority speak volumes about his character.

The centurion's posture—unworthy yet bold, humble yet confident—stands in stark contrast to the entitlement and arrogance that often accompany power. In the world of Roman authority, strength was measured by dominance and control. Yet, this centurion demonstrates a strength of a different kind: the strength to humble himself before Jesus and trust in His word alone.

This moment invites us to reflect on our approach to God. Do we come to Him with a sense of entitlement, pointing to our achievements or perceived worthiness? Or do we, like the centurion, approach with humility, recognizing that all we have is grace? The centurion demonstrates that true faith doesn't presume upon God's favor but boldly trusts in His character and power.

Moreover, the centurion's faith challenges us to consider how we view Jesus's authority. Do we truly believe that His word alone is enough? Or do we, like so many in Jesus's time, insist on seeing tangible evidence before we trust Him? The centurion's bold request— "Say the word"—is a powerful reminder of the sufficiency of Jesus's authority. His faith rests not in what Jesus must do but in who Jesus is.

In this brief yet profound exchange, the centurion exemplifies a faith that amazes. It is a faith that acknowledges unworthiness while stepping forward in bold trust. It is a faith that understands Jesus's power and respects His ways. Moreover, it is a faith that invites us to approach God not with demands or entitlement but with reverence, dependence, and confidence in His word.

Faith in a Word

The centurion's faith reaches its pinnacle in his profound declaration: "But say the word, and let my servant be healed" (Luke 7:7). In this simple statement, the centurion expresses extraordinary trust in Jesus. He believes that Jesus doesn't need to be physically present to perform the miracle. He doesn't ask for a dramatic display, an elaborate ritual, or any outward sign to confirm Jesus's power. Instead, he places his entire confidence in the authority of Jesus's word.

To explain his reasoning, the centurion draws on his own experience with authority: "For I too am a man set under authority, with soldiers under me: and I say to one, 'Go,' and he goes; and to another, 'Come,' and he comes; and to my servant, 'Do this,' and he does it" (Luke 7:8). As a Roman officer, the centurion is deeply familiar with how authority functions. His commands are obeyed not because of his physical presence, but because of the authority vested in him by the empire. His words carry the full weight of Roman power, and his soldiers act accordingly.

This understanding of authority forms the basis of the centurion's faith. He recognizes that Jesus possesses an authority infinitely greater than his own—an authority over sickness, life, and the natural world itself. Just as the centurion's commands are carried out because of the power behind them, he trusts that Jesus's word alone is sufficient to accomplish what He wills. This insight is remarkable. The centurion, a Gentile with no formal connection to the Jewish faith, perceives a truth that many in Israel failed to grasp: Jesus's word carries divine power. It doesn't need reinforcement or proof; it simply needs to be spoken.

The centurion's faith stands in profound contrast to the expectations of many others who encountered Jesus. In the Gospels, we see people demanding signs and wonders, seeking tangible evidence before they believe. Even some of Jesus's own disciples struggled to fully trust His authority without visible proof. Yet this Gentile officer demonstrates a faith that doesn't rely on what can be seen or touched. He trusts in the unseen, confident that Jesus's command will bring healing—even from a distance.

This depth of faith challenges our modern understanding of authority and faith. In a culture that often resists submission to authority, the centurion's recognition of Jesus's divine authority is both refreshing and convicting. True faith, as demonstrated by the centurion, requires more than simply acknowledging Jesus as a teacher or healer. It requires submitting to Him as Lord, trusting that His word holds power over every aspect of our lives.

The centurion's faith also invites us to examine our own response to Jesus's authority. Do we, like the centurion, trust in the sufficiency of Jesus's word? Or do we hesitate, waiting for additional signs or assurances before acting on His commands? Faith is not about controlling outcomes or demanding proof; it is about trusting the One who speaks with ultimate authority.

Moreover, the centurion's declaration reminds us of the sheer power of Jesus's word. In creation, God spoke, and the universe came into existence. In His ministry, Jesus calmed storms, cast out demons, and raised the dead with a single command. The centurion's faith aligns with this biblical truth: Jesus's word is not limited by time, space, or circumstance. When He speaks, reality shifts.

This moment also highlights the humility of true faith. The centurion doesn't presume upon Jesus or demand His intervention. He approaches with boldness and reverence, trusting Jesus's authority while recognizing his unworthiness. This balance of humility and confidence is a hallmark of great faith. The centurion doesn't need to see Jesus's power displayed in a particular way; he simply trusts that Jesus has the authority to act.

The centurion's faith challenges us to trust in Jesus's word, not merely in theory, but in practice. Do we believe that His promises are true and sufficient? Do we act on His commands, confident in His power to accomplish His will? True faith doesn't wait for perfect conditions or visible signs. It rests in Jesus's authority, trusting that His word is enough.

In the centurion's bold yet humble declaration, we see a faith that amazes Jesus—a faith that recognizes His authority, trusts His power, and rests in His word. This is the kind of faith we are called to cultivate: a faith that doesn't require dramatic displays but simply trusts in the One who speaks with the authority of God Himself.

Jesus Marvels

When Jesus hears the centurion's message, He marvels. It is one of the few times in the Gospels where Jesus is described as astonished. Turning to the crowd following Him, Jesus declares, "I tell you, not even in Israel have I found such faith" (Luke 7:9). This statement is both profound and provocative. It highlights not only the centurion's extraordinary faith but also the lack of faith among those who should have been most receptive to Jesus.

The crowd around Jesus primarily consisted of Jewish people—those who had grown up immersed in the promises of God, studying the Scriptures, and anticipating the arrival of the

Messiah. They were heirs to a covenantal relationship with God, supported by generations of stories recounting His faithfulness. Yet, it is a Roman centurion—a Gentile, an outsider, and a representative of the occupying force—who demonstrates the kind of faith that amazes Jesus.

This moment is striking for several reasons. First, it underscores the universal nature of faith. The centurion's ethnicity, status, and religious background are irrelevant to Jesus. What matters is the quality of his faith—a faith that transcends cultural and religious boundaries. By praising the centurion, Jesus shatters the assumptions of His audience. Faith is not confined to those with the right lineage, knowledge, or rituals. It is accessible to anyone who recognizes Jesus's authority and trusts in His word.

Second, Jesus's reaction highlights the contrast between the centurion's faith and the skepticism He often faced among His own people. Many in Israel had witnessed Jesus's miracles, heard His teachings, and even seen prophecies fulfilled in His life. Yet their responses were often marked by doubt, entitlement, or outright rejection. The people of Nazareth, for example, questioned how someone so familiar—a carpenter's son—could be the Messiah (Mark 6:3). The religious leaders, steeped in the Scriptures, often opposed Jesus, blinded by their pride and rigid traditions. In stark contrast, the centurion demonstrates a pure and humble faith that demands no proof, no spectacle, and no conditions. He simply trusts.

Jesus marveling at the centurion's faith is not just a compliment; it is a rebuke to the unbelief He encountered among His own people. His statement—"not even in Israel"—

would have been jarring to those who heard it. It challenged their assumptions about who could have faith and what faith truly looked like. The centurion's example revealed that true faith isn't about proximity to religious traditions or outward displays of piety. It's about recognizing who Jesus is and placing complete trust in Him.

This moment also invites us to reflect on the nature of our own faith. Are we like the centurion, trusting in Jesus's authority and resting in His word, or do we resemble the crowds and religious leaders, hesitant to believe unless our expectations are met? The centurion's faith is remarkable not because of its size or display but because of its simplicity, humility, and clarity. He understood that Jesus's power was not bound by proximity or ritual. He didn't need to see Jesus act to believe that He could.

Finally, Jesus's amazement reminds us that faith moves the heart of God. The centurion's trust and humility elicited an astonished response from the Creator of the universe. This should encourage us to pursue a faith that amazes—not by striving for perfection or trying to prove ourselves, but by humbly recognizing Jesus's authority and trusting Him completely.

The centurion's faith stands as a timeless example. It challenges us to strip away the layers of doubt, pride, and preconditions that often cloud our trust in Jesus. It reminds us that faith isn't about having all the answers or meeting a set of qualifications—it's about looking to Jesus, acknowledging His authority, and believing that His word is enough. And when we do, it's the kind of faith that amazes Him still.

Faith Rewarded

The story reaches its triumphant conclusion with a simple yet profound act: Jesus speaks the word, and the servant is healed. Luke records, "When those who had been sent returned to the house, they found the servant well" (Luke 7:10). There is no dramatic display, no physical touch, and no journey to the centurion's house. Jesus's word alone accomplishes what was impossible for anyone else. It is a quiet yet powerful reminder of the authority of Christ and the sufficiency of faith.

The centurion's faith is rewarded in this moment, but not because of his worthiness or accomplishments. In fact, his earlier declaration— "I am not worthy to have you come under my roof"—reveals that he understood better than most that no one can earn God's help. The centurion's faith was rewarded due to his trust in Jesus, not his merit. This underscores a central truth about faith: it is not about what we bring to God, but about recognizing our need for Him and placing our trust in His power and grace.

This healing also reinforces the authority of Jesus. With a single word spoken from a distance, He restores a dying servant to full health. This moment vividly demonstrates what the centurion already believed: Jesus's power is not bound by physical proximity or human limitations. His authority is absolute, extending over sickness, time, space, and life itself. The healing validates the centurion's trust and confirms what Jesus had marveled at earlier: a faith that sees and submits to divine authority without hesitation or conditions.

The centurion's faith and its reward invite us to examine the nature of our own faith. Do we trust Jesus to work in ways we cannot see or control, or do we cling to the need for visible evidence and immediate results? Faith, as the centurion shows, is not dependent on seeing miracles; it is rooted in confidence in the character and authority of Jesus. The centurion believed that Jesus could heal with a word, and his faith was justified.

This conclusion also speaks to the generous nature of God's grace. Jesus did not heal the servant because of the centurion's good deeds, although they were commendable. The healing was not a transaction or a reward for building a synagogue or loving the Jewish people. Instead, it was an act of grace—a response to the centurion's humble and bold faith. This reinforces the idea that God's help is not earned; it is freely given to those who trust Him.

The story challenges us to consider how we approach God. Do we come to Him with a list of reasons why we think we deserve His help, or do we approach Him in humility, recognizing our unworthiness while trusting in His grace? The centurion's example reminds us that faith is not about impressing God with our worthiness—it's about acknowledging His worthiness and placing our lives in His hands.

Lastly, this story highlights the transformative power of faith. The servant's healing is not just a physical restoration; it offers a glimpse into the greater healing that Jesus provides for all who believe in Him. Just as the centurion's faith brought life to his servant, our faith in Jesus brings spiritual life to us. The servant's healing foreshadows the ultimate restoration that Jesus came to bring—healing for our souls, victory over sin and death, and eternal life with God.

Faith rewarded is not simply about getting what we ask for; it's about experiencing the power and grace of Jesus in ways that deepen our trust in Him. The centurion's story reminds us that when we recognize our need, trust in Jesus's authority, and believe in His word, we open ourselves to the transformative work of God—a work that not only changes circumstances but also reshapes our understanding of who He is and how He works.

Lessons for Us

This story compels us to evaluate the depth and character of our own faith. Do we trust Jesus with the same confidence and humility as the centurion? Are we willing to approach Him not based on our own worthiness, accomplishments, or status, but solely on the basis of His grace? And do we truly believe in the extent of His authority—over every area of our lives, including those situations that feel utterly beyond our control? The centurion's faith challenges us to move beyond a shallow, conditional trust and into a faith that rests fully on Jesus's word and character.

The centurion's example also reminds us of the boundless reach of God's grace. As a Roman soldier, the centurion was an outsider to Israel's covenant community, perceived by many as an enemy or oppressor. Yet, his faith surpassed even those who were immersed in the promises of God from a young age. This story powerfully illustrates that the Gospel is for everyone, regardless of background, status, or ethnicity. Jesus responds to faith, not to pedigree, social standing, or religious affiliation. This inclusiveness challenges any notions of exclusivity we may hold about who is worthy of God's grace. The story of the centurion declares unequivocally that God's kingdom welcomes all who come to Him in faith.

Another profound lesson from this passage is the inseparable connection between humility and genuine faith. The centurion could have approached Jesus with arrogance or entitlement, leveraging his rank and accomplishments to demand help. After all, even the Jewish elders had deemed him "worthy" of Jesus's intervention based on his deeds. But the centurion didn't buy into their assessment. Instead, he came with a profound awareness of his own unworthiness, acknowledging that he was not even fit to have Jesus enter his home.

Far from weakening his faith, this humility strengthened it. The centurion's awareness of his own limitations deepened his dependence on Jesus's authority and mercy. True humility doesn't diminish faith; it clears the way for it. It allows us to recognize that our hope doesn't rest in what we bring to the table but entirely in who Jesus is. This humility enabled the centurion to trust Jesus's word without hesitation, even from a distance. His faith wasn't hindered by pride or a sense of entitlement; it was empowered by his understanding of his own need and Jesus's sufficiency.

This story also challenges our cultural assumptions about power and control. The centurion was a man of significant authority, yet he recognized that his power had limits. When faced with a situation beyond his control, he didn't cling to his status or influence but instead turned to Jesus, whose authority was absolute. This is a convicting reminder for those of us who are accustomed to relying on our own resources, plans, or positions of influence. Do we, like the centurion, have the humility to admit when we are powerless and the faith to entrust those moments to Jesus?

Lastly, the centurion's faith encourages us to reflect on the nature of Jesus's authority in our lives. Do we truly believe that His authority extends over everything—our health, our relationships, our future, and even the areas of our lives we try to keep hidden? Faith like the centurion's recognizes that there is no part of life too small or too vast for Jesus's power and care. It acknowledges that His word is sufficient, even when circumstances feel overwhelming.

The centurion's story is not just a testimony of faith—it's a challenge to cultivate a faith marked by humility, dependence, and trust in Jesus's word. It invites us to see beyond ourselves, to embrace the radical inclusivity of God's grace, and to rest in the unshakable authority of Christ. When we approach Jesus with this kind of faith, we too can experience the transformative power of His word and His presence in our lives.

REFLECTION QUESTIONS:

1. **How does the centurion's humility challenge the way you approach Jesus?** Are there areas in your life where pride or entitlement might be hindering your faith?

2. The centurion believed that Jesus's authority extended over everything, even sickness. **Do you trust that Jesus has authority over every part of your life, including the areas that feel out of control?**

3. The centurion's faith amazed Jesus. **What would it look like to cultivate a faith that pleases and honors Him?**

4. This story shows that God's grace is for everyone, regardless of background or status. **How can you reflect this truth in the way you interact with others?**

5. The centurion's faith was rooted in Jesus's word. **How can you grow in trusting and applying the promises of God's word in your daily life?**

CHAPTER 4:
FAITH AND FRIENDSHIP

What would you do to get to Jesus? Or better yet, what would you be willing to do to bring someone you loved to Him? These questions reveal our priorities, expose what we believe about Jesus, and challenge our willingness to sacrifice for others. In Mark 2:1-12, four friends provide a compelling answer. Faced with obstacles, they didn't give up—they broke through. Their story challenges us to consider what real faith looks like and how it acts, not just for our own needs but also for the needs of others.

This story is about more than a paralyzed man. It's about the faith of his friends and their determination to bring him to Jesus, the only one who could heal him. Their faith wasn't passive—it was bold, persistent, and sacrificial. Climbing onto a roof, digging through it, and lowering their friend into Jesus's presence demonstrated a trust that overcame every barrier. Their actions remind us that true faith isn't just belief—it's belief in action.

Jesus's response to their faith is unexpected. Instead of healing the man immediately, He says, "Son, your sins are forgiven" (Mark 2:5). Jesus addresses the deeper issue—spiritual paralysis. This challenges us to consider how often we focus on external problems while neglecting deeper spiritual needs. Jesus sees what we cannot and meets us at the root of our brokenness.

When Jesus forgives the man's sins, He also reveals His authority, provoking outrage from the religious leaders. To prove His power, He commands the man to rise, and the paralyzed man walks out, restored both physically and spiritually. This moment confirms that Jesus's authority extends over every aspect of life—physical, emotional, and spiritual.

Finally, this story challenges us to bring others to Jesus. The friends' intercessory faith reminds us of our role in removing barriers for those who need Him. Who in our lives needs Jesus? What are we willing to do to bring them to Him? This story isn't just about faith—it's about faith that acts, trusts, and loves boldly, knowing that Jesus is the only one who can heal and restore.

Friends Who Love Boldly

The story begins with Jesus returning to Capernaum. Word spreads quickly, and soon the house where He's staying is packed to capacity. People cram into every corner, spill out the doorway, and line up outside, straining to hear Him teach. The crowd is so dense that it creates a human barrier, making it impossible for anyone else to get through (Mark 2:1-2).

Enter the friends, carrying a paralyzed man on a mat. Their mission is clear: get their friend to Jesus. But this isn't just a logistical challenge—it's a deeply compassionate act. In the ancient world, paralysis was more than a physical condition; it carried social and spiritual stigma. Disabilities were often seen as evidence of sin or divine punishment, leaving people not only physically incapacitated but also socially ostracized. These friends didn't merely address a physical need; they stood in solidarity with someone whom society had pushed to the margins.

When they arrive and see the impenetrable crowd, they face a crucial moment of decision. Most people might have given up, reasoning that the circumstances were beyond their control. "We tried," they could have said. "It's too crowded. Maybe another time." But not these friends. Their love for their companion and their faith in Jesus propels them forward. They refuse to let the crowd, the logistics, or even social norms stop them. They climb onto the roof, tear it apart, and lower their friend directly in front of Jesus (Mark 2:3-4).

Their actions are bold, even audacious. Tearing apart a roof wasn't a quiet or subtle act—it caused noise, disruption, and likely showered debris on the crowd below. It was risky and inconvenient, potentially drawing criticism or anger from the homeowner and others. However, their focus wasn't on the potential fallout; it was on the hope that Jesus could heal their friend.

This raises a question that confronts all of us: How far are we willing to go for those we love? Are we prepared to inconvenience ourselves, disrupt others, or risk rejection to bring someone closer to Jesus? These friends remind us that real love is active and persistent. It doesn't stop at good intentions; it takes bold, sometimes messy steps to ensure that those we care about have the opportunity to encounter Christ.

Their example challenges us to examine the depth of our own faith and love. Do we trust Jesus enough to act on behalf of others? Are we willing to step out of our comfort zones to meet not just their physical needs but also their deeper spiritual ones? The friends' determination shows that love isn't afraid to get its hands dirty when the stakes are high. They understood that the cost of their effort paled in comparison to the hope of what Jesus could do. And in their radical love and faith, they cleared the way for a life-changing encounter.

Barriers That Expose Belief

When the friends encounter the crowd, they are forced to make a pivotal choice: turn back or find another way. Their determination to press forward reveals the depth of their faith and what they truly believe about Jesus—that He is worth any effort. Barriers have a way of exposing what we value most. If something matters enough, we'll find a way; if it doesn't, we'll find an excuse. For these friends, the thought of their companion missing an opportunity to be healed by Jesus is unthinkable. Their resolve demonstrates a faith that isn't deterred by difficulty but grows stronger in the face of it.

The crowd itself is an intriguing element in the story. These people weren't hostile or antagonistic—they were there to hear Jesus teach, likely seeking healing or guidance for themselves. Yet their presence unintentionally created a barrier, preventing others from reaching Jesus. This raises a convicting question for us: How often are we like that crowd? How often, in our eagerness to experience Jesus for ourselves, do we unintentionally block others from coming to Him? It's easy to become so consumed with our own needs or preoccupied with our personal encounters with Jesus that we fail to notice those who need help getting to Him. Worse yet, sometimes our indifference, judgmental attitudes, or even clinging to comfort and routine create obstacles for others.

The friends' response to this barrier is both inspiring and instructive. They don't waste time blaming the crowd, making excuses, or passively waiting for circumstances to change. Instead, they act. Their creativity and determination serve as a powerful example of what real faith looks like. Faith isn't passive; it's persistent. It doesn't retreat when faced with obstacles but instead adapts and presses forward. The friends' decision to climb onto the roof, tear it apart, and lower their companion into Jesus's presence is a striking picture of bold, relentless faith. Their actions reveal a deep conviction that getting to Jesus is worth any inconvenience, risk, or disruption.

The friends' boldness also highlights the sacrificial nature of true love. They weren't just motivated by faith—they were driven by love for their paralyzed companion. Their willingness to face obstacles, disrupt the scene, and potentially embarrass themselves underscores the lengths they were willing to go for someone they cared about. This challenges us to reflect on the depth of our own love for those around us. Are we willing to inconvenience ourselves, take risks, or make sacrifices to bring others to Jesus? Do we share the same urgency and determination to see others encounter Him?

Barriers also challenge us personally. Do we allow obstacles in our lives to keep us from Jesus, or do we respond with the same persistence these friends displayed? Faith often requires boldness and creativity, especially when faced with resistance, whether internal or external. Sometimes, barriers are opportunities in disguise, moments that test the depth of our trust and refine the strength of our faith.

Ultimately, the barriers in this story act as a mirror, reflecting both the strength of the friends' faith and the subtle ways we can obstruct or be obstructed in our journey to Jesus. Their determination to overcome the crowd underscores a simple yet profound truth: real faith doesn't stop at obstacles—it finds a way to Jesus, no matter what it takes. In doing so, it clears the path for others to experience the transformative power of Christ.

Jesus Confronts the Heart of the Matter

As the paralyzed man is lowered through the roof, all eyes turn to Jesus. Dust likely still lingers in the air, and fragments of clay and thatch are scattered on the ground, creating an electric atmosphere filled with anticipation. The crowd, pressed tightly together, holds its breath, expecting to witness another dramatic display of healing power. But what Jesus says next shocks everyone: "Son, your sins are forgiven" (Mark 2:5).

This declaration must have felt confusing, even frustrating, to the man's friends. After all, they had just gone to extraordinary lengths to bring him to Jesus for a physical cure. Imagine their thoughts: *"Forgiveness? That's not why we're here. We didn't break through a roof for that—we came for a miracle!"* Yet Jesus sees what no one else does. He understands that the man's paralysis, as painful and life-altering as it is, is not his greatest need. His deepest problem is not physical but spiritual. The man needs reconciliation with God more than he needs the ability to walk.

Jesus's response reveals something profound about the priorities of the kingdom of God and the condition of the human heart. We often focus on the external, the immediate, and the visible while neglecting the internal and eternal realities of our souls. The man's friends were consumed with his inability to walk, and likely he himself had longed for nothing more than to regain his mobility. But Jesus goes straight to the root of the issue. He doesn't dismiss the man's physical suffering; instead, He addresses the deeper, eternal problem first: the man's sin and separation from God.

This moment is a powerful reminder that Jesus always sees beneath the surface. While the crowd is fixated on the man's external condition, Jesus gazes into his heart. He understands that physical healing, though miraculous, would only address a temporary problem. The man could regain the ability to walk, but without forgiveness, he would remain spiritually paralyzed—alienated from God and unable to experience true life.

By prioritizing the man's spiritual need, Jesus challenges the assumptions of everyone in the room, including us. How often do we come to Jesus primarily seeking relief from external problems, whether physical illness, financial struggles, or relational conflict, while neglecting the deeper issues of the heart? This moment reminds us that Jesus is always concerned with what matters most—our relationship with God.

Jesus's declaration also sets the stage for a confrontation with the religious leaders present. To them, this statement is not just surprising; it's blasphemous. "Who can forgive sins but God alone?" they silently accuse (Mark 2:7). Their reaction reveals a critical truth: Jesus's claim to forgive sins is a direct assertion of

His divine authority. He is not just a healer or teacher—He is God in the flesh, possessing the power to restore both body and soul.

This moment encompasses far more than one man's healing. It reveals who Jesus is and what He came to accomplish. His mission is not merely to fix what is broken in the world but to reconcile humanity with God. The forgiveness Jesus offers is not just an add-on to His ministry—it is the very heart of it. By addressing the man's sin first, Jesus clarifies that the kingdom of God is about more than physical restoration; it's about the restoration of the soul.

In this seemingly simple declaration, Jesus reorients our understanding of what we truly need. We often come to Him with our immediate problems, expecting solutions to our external struggles, but He gently redirects our attention to the deeper issues of our hearts. His words remind us that while He cares deeply about our physical and emotional needs, His ultimate priority is our spiritual restoration.

This moment invites us to examine our own hearts. What are we bringing to Jesus? Are we primarily seeking temporary relief, or are we open to the deeper, transformative work He wants to do in our lives? The friends lowered their companion through the roof for a miracle, but Jesus gave them something far greater: a glimpse of the kingdom of God and the hope of total restoration. In addressing the heart of the matter, Jesus shows us that what we need most is not just healing—it's Him.

Sin is the Deeper Problem

Jesus isn't dismissing the man's physical suffering; rather, He's exposing the deeper issue. Sin, more than any physical ailment, is the root cause of all brokenness in the world. It separates us from God, distorts our relationships, and fractures our souls. While paralysis might confine the man's body, sin enslaves his soul—and that is a far greater tragedy.

By addressing sin first, Jesus teaches a profound truth: our deepest problems are not external but internal. Paralysis, as painful and limiting as it is, is only a symptom of a much larger issue. Sin is the underlying disease that infects every aspect of life and creation. This man's inability to walk is a significant burden, but Jesus knows that his greatest need is reconciliation with God. Without forgiveness, even a healed body remains bound by the deeper chains of spiritual separation.

This moment challenges our priorities and perspectives. We often come to Jesus primarily seeking solutions to immediate, visible problems—relief from pain, provision in hardship, or help in crisis. While these needs are real and important, Jesus shows us that they are not ultimate. Physical healing can improve circumstances, but forgiveness restores the soul and mends our relationship with God. It addresses the eternal need that underpins every other form of brokenness.

Jesus's words don't diminish the importance of physical suffering; they elevate the need for spiritual transformation. What good would it do for this man to walk again if his soul remained bound by sin? A restored body without a restored soul would still leave him alienated from God, trapped in the deeper paralysis of guilt and separation. Jesus's decision to forgive first reminds us that the kingdom of God is not just about addressing temporary struggles but about offering lasting hope and ultimate restoration.

This truth also speaks to the broader brokenness we see in the world. Every form of suffering—whether physical, emotional, relational, or systemic—can ultimately be traced back to the reality of sin. While acts of compassion, healing, and justice are vital, they are not enough on their own. Without addressing the root cause, the cycle of brokenness will continue. This is why forgiveness is central to Jesus's mission. It's not just about removing the symptoms of sin; it's about curing the disease.

This moment invites us to examine our own hearts. Are we primarily focused on the external problems in our lives, or are we willing to confront the deeper issues within? Do we see Jesus as a means to temporary relief, or do we trust Him to bring the kind of transformation that begins with forgiveness and leads to eternal life? Jesus's words to the paralyzed man remind us that while He cares deeply about every aspect of our suffering, His ultimate goal is to restore us to God, the source of true healing and wholeness.

Jesus Prioritizes What Matters Most

By forgiving the man's sins, Jesus reveals that His mission extends beyond alleviating suffering to addressing the root problem of sin. While physical healing clearly matters to Him—He heals the man later—Jesus shows that forgiveness is the foundation for all true restoration. Without spiritual healing, no other remedy can be complete.

This moment challenges us to reconsider how we approach Jesus. Do we seek Him mainly for external fixes, treating Him like a repairman for our circumstances? Or do we come with humility, asking Him to address the deeper issues within us?

Jesus's actions remind us that while He cares deeply about our struggles, His ultimate goal is spiritual transformation. He invites us to prioritize what matters most: reconciliation with God. Through forgiveness, Jesus offers a healing that begins in the heart and changes everything else.

A Challenge to Our Priorities

Jesus's response to the paralyzed man challenges us to examine our own priorities. We often approach Him asking for relief from external struggles—healing from illness, financial provision, reconciliation in relationships. These are good and necessary concerns to bring to Him; Jesus invites us to cast all our cares upon Him. But do we stop there? Are we more focused on having our circumstances changed than allowing Him to transform us?

Jesus's words remind us that while external problems feel urgent, they are not our deepest issues. The greater tragedy would be to walk away from Jesus with our circumstances improved but our hearts unchanged. His first words to the man—"Your sins are forgiven"—are a profound invitation to reorient our focus. Jesus calls us to bring not only the visible struggles of our lives but also the unseen brokenness of our hearts.

This moment urges us to confront an uncomfortable question: Do we truly want the kind of healing Jesus offers, or are we more interested in temporary fixes? His response to the paralyzed man challenges us to trust Him with our most pressing needs while also surrendering the hidden parts of ourselves—the sin, the fear, the shame—to the One who can bring lasting transformation. Through His words, Jesus points us to what matters most: a restored relationship with God that addresses the ultimate source of all brokenness.

Transforming How We See Jesus

This moment reframes how we understand Jesus. He isn't just a miracle worker or healer; He's the Savior. While the crowd was likely fixated on His ability to heal physical ailments, Jesus uses this opportunity to reveal something far greater: His authority to forgive sins. By addressing the man's spiritual need first, Jesus demonstrates His ultimate mission. He didn't come merely to fix what's broken on the surface; He came to reconcile humanity to God and restore what sin has destroyed.

This story invites us to examine how we view Jesus. Do we approach Him primarily as a problem-solver—someone who can alleviate our struggles and make life more comfortable? Or do we see Him as the Savior who offers true and lasting transformation? It's not wrong to seek His help in times of need; Jesus welcomes our burdens. However, His words to the paralyzed man challenge us to look beyond temporary relief and recognize the eternal healing He offers.

Jesus's actions remind us that His work goes deeper than we often expect or even desire. He isn't merely interested in improving our circumstances; He's interested in saving our souls. This moment calls us to trust Him not just as a provider for our immediate needs but as the one who has the power to redeem and transform every part of our lives. It shifts our focus from what we think we need to what we truly need: the forgiveness, grace, and new life that only Jesus can give.

Religious Resistance

Not everyone in the room is impressed by Jesus's words. The scribes, who are experts in Jewish law, are outraged. They think to themselves, "Why does this man speak like that? He is blaspheming! Who can forgive sins but God alone?" (Mark 2:6-7). Their reaction reveals their deep misunderstanding of Jesus's identity and their own spiritual blindness.

To their credit, the scribes aren't entirely wrong. The forgiveness of sins is indeed the prerogative of God alone. What they miss, however, is the radical truth unfolding before their eyes. The very God they revere stands in front of them in human form. Jesus's claim to forgive sins is not blasphemy; it's a revelation of His divine authority.

But the scribes can't see it. Their hearts are hardened, their minds are closed, and their traditions have become barriers to recognizing the truth. For years, they studied the Scriptures, memorized the law, and awaited the Messiah. Yet when the Messiah appears, they reject Him because He doesn't fit their expectations. They are so focused on preserving their own power and theological categories that they miss the grace of God at work.

This resistance isn't unique to the scribes; it's a human problem. How often do we reject what God is doing because it doesn't align with our expectations? How often do we cling to our own understanding instead of humbly submitting to His authority? The scribes' reaction is a warning against the dangers of pride, self-righteousness, and spiritual complacency.

Their resistance also reveals the depth of their unbelief. They see Jesus perform miracles, hear His authoritative teaching, and witness His compassion, yet they accuse Him of blasphemy. This isn't a lack of evidence; it's a refusal to believe. The scribes have placed themselves as judges over Jesus, evaluating Him based on their own limited understanding. But the irony is that Jesus is the ultimate judge, and their rejection of Him only exposes their own spiritual blindness.

What's sobering about the scribes' response is that they are the religious insiders. They should have been the first to recognize and celebrate Jesus as the fulfillment of God's promises. Instead, they become obstacles to others encountering Him. This compels us to ask: Are there ways we, as followers of Christ, unintentionally become like the scribes? Do we create barriers for others through our attitudes, assumptions, or actions?

The scribes' resistance highlights the need for humility and openness in our faith. It reminds us that true spiritual sight comes not from our own efforts or intellect, but from a heart willing to see and receive Jesus for who He truly is.

Authority That Heals and Forgives

Jesus doesn't leave the scribes' doubts and accusations unaddressed. He confronts them directly with a bold question: "Why do you question these things in your hearts? Which is easier, to say to the paralytic, 'Your sins are forgiven,' or to say, 'Rise, take up your bed and walk'?" (Mark 2:8-9).

This question is profound and challenging. On the surface, it might seem easier to say, "Your sins are forgiven," because there's no visible way to verify whether it has actually happened. However, Jesus knows that forgiveness is not a cheap declaration. It requires divine authority and the ultimate cost—His own sacrifice on the cross. By asking this question, Jesus draws attention to the fact that He has the authority to do both: forgive sins and heal the body.

To prove His authority, Jesus turns to the paralyzed man and says, "I say to you, rise, pick up your bed, and go home" (Mark 2:11). Instantly, the man stands up, picks up his mat, and walks out in full view of everyone. The crowd is amazed, and they glorify God, saying, "We never saw anything like this!" (Mark 2:12).

This miracle isn't just about the man's physical healing; it's a public demonstration of Jesus's authority. By healing the man, Jesus provides visible evidence that He has the power to forgive sins. The physical act of making a paralyzed man walk points to the spiritual reality of His divine nature. It's as if Jesus is saying, "If I can do this in the physical realm, imagine what I can do in the spiritual realm."

Jesus's authority extends beyond what we can see or comprehend. He doesn't just heal symptoms; He addresses root causes. He doesn't just meet temporary needs; He offers eternal solutions. In healing the man's paralysis, Jesus demonstrates that His power isn't limited to the physical world. He is Lord over both body and soul, time and eternity.

This moment also reveals the depth of Jesus's compassion. He doesn't just see a paralyzed man; He sees a person made in the image of God, broken by sin but deeply loved. He doesn't just respond to the friends' faith; He acts out of His own divine love and purpose. Jesus's authority is never detached from His compassion. The same power that forgives and heals is driven by a heart that longs to restore.

What's striking about this miracle is how it reframes our understanding of what true healing means. The crowd likely focused on the man's physical condition, but Jesus concentrated on his spiritual state. The man walked away not only with restored legs but also with a restored relationship with God. This challenges us to think about what we truly need from Jesus. Do we come to Him seeking only relief from our circumstances, or do we trust Him to address the deeper issues of our hearts?

Jesus's authority also confronts us with a decision. If He truly has the power to forgive sins and heal brokenness, then He is Lord, and we owe Him our full allegiance. But if we reject His authority, we are left with our own brokenness and the weight of our sin. There is no middle ground. The miracle in this story demands a response—not just from the scribes and the crowd but from us as well.

Faith That Transforms

The friends' faith in this story is not only inspiring but also transformative. Their love for their paralyzed friend compels them to take bold and creative action. This is faith in motion—faith that believes so deeply in Jesus's power that it pushes past every obstacle. Their faith transforms the story, resulting in both a visible miracle and a deeper spiritual truth.

This wasn't an individual faith; it was communal, shared among the friends who worked together to bring the man to Jesus. Faith like this reminds us that we need each other. Sometimes we're the ones carrying others to Jesus, and other times we're the ones being carried. Both roles require humility, love, and trust.

Their persistence in the face of barriers shows that true faith doesn't give up. They didn't wait for the crowd to part or for circumstances to change; instead, they found another way. Transformative faith is both creative and determined because it understands that Jesus is worth the effort. It doesn't shrink back at the first sign of difficulty but presses on, believing that He can and will act.

Finally, these friends' faith was contagious. Their bold actions didn't just heal the paralyzed man; they caused the entire crowd to glorify God (Mark 2:12). True faith draws others to Jesus. It points beyond itself to the Savior, inviting everyone to see His power and compassion.

Transformative faith brings people into Jesus's presence, trusting Him to do what only He can do. It doesn't settle for surface-level change; it seeks the kind of deep, lasting restoration that only He offers. This is the kind of faith that not only moves mountains but also changes lives forever.

Who Are You in the Story?

This story invites us to see ourselves in its characters. Are we like the friends, willing to do whatever it takes to bring others to Jesus, even at great personal cost? Their love, creativity, and determination reflect a faith that doesn't quit. Are we like the paralyzed man, unable to make it to Jesus on our own, in need of someone to carry us, yet willing to trust Him with our deepest brokenness? Or are we like the scribes, skeptical and resistant to the idea that Jesus has the authority to transform lives—perhaps even ours?

The truth is, we've probably been all three at different points in our lives. Sometimes we're the friends, acting in bold faith to help others encounter Jesus. At times, we're the paralyzed man, burdened by our own brokenness and relying on the faith and support of others. And, if we are honest, there are moments when we are the scribes, standing on the sidelines with folded arms, allowing doubt or pride to block us from seeing who Jesus truly is.

But here's the good news: Jesus meets us wherever we are. He doesn't wait for us to figure it all out or fix ourselves first. Whether we're carrying others, being carried, or wrestling with doubt, His invitation is the same: Trust Him. Bring your questions, your burdens, your fears, and your faith—no matter how small—and let Him do what only He can do. In His presence, there's forgiveness for the doubter, healing for the broken, and strength for the one stepping out in faith. Whatever role you find yourself in, Jesus is ready to meet you there.

REFLECTION QUESTIONS

1. **What barriers in your life are keeping you from fully trusting Jesus?** How can you overcome them?

2. **Who in your life needs you to act like the friends in this story?** How can you bring them to Jesus this week?

3. **Are there ways you've unintentionally created barriers for others to encounter Jesus?** How can you remove them?

4. What does Jesus's willingness to address the man's spiritual needs first teach you about His priorities?

5. How can your faith grow to be more persistent, creative, and unrelenting like the friends in this story?

CHAPTER 5:
THE ONE THING YOU WON'T LET GO

What is the one thing keeping you from following Jesus completely? If Jesus stood before you today and asked for it, would you let it go? It's easy to say "yes" in theory, but what about in reality? We all have something—a relationship, a goal, a possession, a sense of control—that holds our hearts more tightly than we'd like to admit. And that one thing, whatever it may be, has the power to keep us from fully experiencing the life Jesus offers.

In Mark 10:17-27, we meet a man who had everything—wealth, influence, moral integrity, and ambition. Yet, in the most important moment of his life, he walks away from Jesus, grieving. Why? Because the one thing he couldn't let go of was the very thing standing between him and eternal life. This isn't just a story about a rich man; it's a story about all of us. We all wrestle with idols that compete for our ultimate allegiance.

The rich young ruler's encounter with Jesus is both inspiring and heartbreaking. He approaches with urgency, running to Jesus. He kneels, showing reverence, and asks a question that many of us have wondered at some point in our lives: "What must I do to inherit eternal life?" His actions suggest that he's genuinely seeking truth. Yet, as the story unfolds, we discover that his heart is tethered to something he values more than Jesus.

This passage isn't just about wealth; it's about worship. It's not just about possessions; it's about priorities. It's not just about surrendering what we have; it's about discovering who Jesus is and why He's worth it. Mark 10:17-27 confronts us with the radical nature of discipleship. It forces us to ask: What am I unwilling to let go of, and what does that say about my relationship with Christ?

At its core, this story is about treasure. The rich young ruler treasured his wealth, but Jesus calls him to treasure something far greater: Himself. It's a call to leave behind the fleeting pleasures of this world and embrace the eternal joy of following Christ. As we walk through this passage, we'll see that Jesus doesn't just ask for everything; He offers everything. He isn't trying to take from us—He's trying to give us something infinitely better. The question is, will we trust Him enough to let go of the one thing keeping us from Him?

A Burning Question

The story begins with a sense of urgency that's hard to ignore. The rich young ruler doesn't saunter up to Jesus or wait for a quiet moment to speak with Him. He comes running, a picture of eagerness, desperation, and determination. He falls to his knees—a striking display of humility, especially for a man of his wealth and status. This isn't a casual encounter; it's the act of someone who knows he's in the presence of someone extraordinary. His actions suggest he recognizes Jesus as more than just another rabbi, but his words reveal how much he still misunderstands.

"Good Teacher, what must I do to inherit eternal life?" (Mark 10:17). His question is as significant as his posture. It's one of the most important questions a person can ask, reflecting a concern for eternity and a desire to know the way to God. This man's approach seems genuine, unlike the Pharisees, who often came to Jesus with ulterior motives. He's not here to trap Jesus in His words; he's here because he truly wants to know how to secure eternal life.

But beneath this sincere question lies a dangerous assumption: that eternal life is something he can achieve through his own efforts. The very way he phrases the question— "What must I do?"—reveals that he views eternal life as a transaction. He sees it as something to be earned, another box to check on the list of his accomplishments. This mindset is common even today. Many of us approach God similarly, thinking we can work our way into His favor. We strive to pray more, serve more, and give more, hoping it will be enough. But how much is enough? When have we done enough to secure eternal life? The young ruler is grappling with these very questions.

Jesus's response is both brilliant and provocative: "Why do you call me good? No one is good except God alone" (Mark 10:18). At first glance, this might seem like Jesus is sidestepping the question, but He's doing the opposite. He addresses the core of the man's misunderstanding. By challenging the ruler's use of the word "good," Jesus points to the deeper issue: the man's flawed view of goodness itself.

The young ruler believes that goodness is something attainable through human effort, a standard he can reach if he tries hard enough. But Jesus immediately redirects the conversation. He isn't denying His own goodness or divinity; instead, He invites the ruler to reconsider what true goodness is. If only God is good, then the ruler's efforts to earn eternal life will always fall short. This is a vital moment in the conversation, as Jesus gently but firmly begins to dismantle the man's self-reliance.

In this response, Jesus reveals a profound truth: eternal life isn't a reward for good behavior; it's a gift from a good God. The rich young ruler doesn't need a list of more good deeds to perform; he needs to confront his own inability to achieve perfection and recognize his need for grace. However, that realization is not easy to come to. It requires humility and a willingness to admit that no matter how good we think we are, we're not good enough to bridge the gap between ourselves and God.

How often do we find ourselves in the same position as this young man? We may not phrase the question exactly the same way, but we often ask it in our hearts: "What must I do to be good enough? How can I earn God's approval?" We treat God's favor as something transactional, believing that if we do enough or sacrifice enough, we can secure our standing before Him. Yet, Jesus's words confront us with the same reality He presents to the ruler: no one is truly good except God.

This response isn't meant to discourage us; it's meant to liberate us. It frees us from the exhausting pursuit of earning what only God can give. The rich young ruler doesn't need to do more; he needs to let go of the illusion that he can save himself. The same is true for us. Jesus isn't looking for our perfection—

He's inviting us to rest in His. Eternal life isn't a transaction; it's a relationship with the One who alone is truly good.

A Checklist of Goodness

To meet the man where he is, Jesus begins by listing a series of commandments: "Do not murder, Do not commit adultery, Do not steal, Do not bear false witness, Do not defraud, Honor your father and mother" (Mark 10:19). These are all outward, measurable commands—visible actions that reflect moral behavior in society. For someone like the rich young ruler, these commands likely formed the basis of his understanding of righteousness. He could measure his life against them and confidently say he had lived up to the standard.

The young man eagerly responds, "Teacher, all these I have kept from my youth" (Mark 10:20). There's no hint of arrogance in his answer. He's sincere, disciplined, and committed to doing what is right. By all appearances, he's the kind of person we'd look up to—a model of moral integrity. Yet, despite his best efforts to follow the rules, he knows something is missing. His good deeds haven't given him the assurance he's seeking. His question— "What must I do to inherit eternal life?"—betrays a lingering sense of incompleteness, a gnawing emptiness that even his spotless moral record cannot fill.

This moment resonates with many of us. How often do we find ourselves in the same place? We attend church, read our Bibles, volunteer, give generously, and avoid obvious sins. We check all the boxes, yet still feel an ache, wondering if we've done enough. It's a profoundly human experience—doing all the right things but still sensing that something isn't quite right within us.

What's striking in this exchange is what Jesus does next. He doesn't rebuke the young man for his answer or question the sincerity of his efforts. Instead, Mark tells us something remarkable: "Jesus, looking at him, loved him" (Mark 10:21). In that moment, Jesus sees the man fully—his sincerity, his longing, his misplaced confidence—and He loves him. This is a love that doesn't diminish the man's achievements or dismiss his efforts, but also doesn't leave him comfortable in them. It's a love that challenges and confronts because it desires what is truly best for him.

This is the kind of love Jesus offers to all of us. He sees past our outward displays of morality and into the depths of our hearts. He knows the fears and insecurities we try to mask with good deeds. He knows the idols we cling to, even when we can't name them ourselves. And because He loves us, He doesn't leave us there. His love isn't passive; it's active, calling us out of the false security of our self-righteousness and into the freedom of true discipleship.

The young man's response to Jesus is a mirror for our own struggles. It's easy to equate obedience to rules with spiritual maturity, thinking that checking off a moral checklist is the same as following Christ. However, this story challenges that assumption. Jesus is about to show the rich young ruler—and us—that true righteousness isn't about keeping score. It's about surrender. It's about letting go of the one thing we trust more than God, the one thing we look to for identity, security, or worth.

This passage also exposes the limits of external obedience. The commandments Jesus lists are all relational—they deal with how we treat others. While the young man might have perfectly kept these in his actions, his heart still isn't fully aligned with God. He's missing the greater commandment: to love the Lord with all his heart, soul, mind, and strength (Mark 12:30). External righteousness without internal transformation falls short of the kingdom of God.

In loving the man, Jesus reveals the heart of discipleship. Love doesn't settle for surface-level change; it seeks deep, lasting transformation. It doesn't leave us comfortable in our idols or our illusions of self-sufficiency. Instead, it calls us to let go of whatever holds us back from fully trusting in Jesus. And that's what Jesus is about to ask of this man—not because He wants to take something from him, but because He wants to give him something far greater.

The One Thing You Lack

In a single sentence, Jesus lays bare the idol that rules the rich young ruler's heart: "You lack one thing: go, sell all that you have and give to the poor, and you will have treasure in heaven; and come, follow me" (Mark 10:21). It's a surgical strike, cutting straight to the heart of the man's problem. Wealth isn't just a possession for this man—it's his identity, security, and god. His riches define him, provide comfort and status, and serve as the foundation of his sense of worth. It's the one thing he won't let go of, and it's the very thing keeping him from Jesus.

Notice the precision of Jesus's challenge. He doesn't issue a generalized statement about wealth or possessions; He pinpoints the exact barrier standing between this man and discipleship. Jesus knows that this man's problem isn't just that he has wealth—it's that his wealth has him. It owns his heart, directing his affections and decisions. Jesus's command to sell everything and give to the poor is not a universal call for all believers to divest themselves of their possessions, but rather it is a universal call to confront whatever idol prevents us from fully surrendering to Him. For this man, it's wealth. For others, it might be success, reputation, relationships, or control. Whatever occupies the throne of our hearts must be dethroned if Jesus is to be our King.

Jesus's words are not harsh but deeply loving. Mark tells us, "Jesus, looking at him, loved him" (Mark 10:21). This love isn't permissive or passive; it's the love of a surgeon who cuts precisely to remove what is killing the patient. Jesus doesn't ask the man to sell everything because He wants to make his life harder. He asks it because He wants to set him free. The man's attachment to his wealth is enslaving him, and Jesus knows he'll never experience true freedom, joy, or eternal life until he lets it go.

An Idol That Demands Everything

Idols are never harmless; they always demand everything. They promise satisfaction but deliver emptiness. For the rich young ruler, wealth was not merely a tool or resource—it was his ultimate source of security and significance. Jesus's challenge reveals that the man trusts his possessions more than he trusts God. He can't imagine a life without his wealth, even if it means forfeiting the eternal life he desires.

This moment forces us to ask: What is the one thing we won't let go of? What is the idol that grips our hearts, convincing us that we can't live without it? It might not be money. It could be a career that we've built our identity on, a relationship we fear losing, or even a dream that has become more important to us than following Jesus. Whatever it is, Jesus's invitation is the same: "Let it go. Trust me. Follow me."

A Heartbreaking Response

The rich young ruler's response is one of the most heartbreaking moments in the Gospels: "Disheartened by the saying, he went away sorrowful, for he had great possessions" (Mark 10:22). The man who ran to Jesus, knelt before Him, and asked about eternal life now walks away grieving. Why? Because the cost of following Jesus was too high. He wanted eternal life, but he wanted his wealth more.

This response shows us the power of idols to blind us to the beauty of Christ. The rich young ruler stands face-to-face with the Savior of the world, the One who can give him eternal life, joy, and treasure in heaven, but his heart is so tethered to his possessions that he can't say yes. His grief reveals the truth: idols enslave us. They demand our allegiance and rob us of the freedom Jesus offers. He came to Jesus asking for life, but he couldn't accept the terms of discipleship—complete surrender.

Treasure in Heaven

Jesus's command to "sell all that you have and give to the poor" is not simply about charity or self-denial; it's about exchange. Jesus isn't asking the man to trade something valuable for something worthless; he's asking him to exchange temporary wealth for eternal treasure. "You will have treasure in heaven," Jesus promises (Mark 10:21). This is not a loss but a gain—a gain so immeasurably greater than anything the man could ever accumulate on earth. However, the rich young ruler can't see it. His vision is clouded by his attachment to the here and now.

This moment challenges us to examine where we place our treasure. Jesus once said, "Where your treasure is, there your heart will be also" (Matthew 6:21). The rich young ruler's treasure was on earth, and that's where his heart stayed. But Jesus offers us a treasure that cannot be stolen, destroyed, or diminished—a treasure that satisfies the deepest longings of our hearts because it is found in Him.

The Beauty of Jesus's Call

What makes this encounter so powerful—and so convicting—is that Jesus's call is not just to give up wealth but to follow Him. The rich young ruler isn't being asked to lead a life of misery and deprivation; he's being invited into a life of joy, freedom, and intimacy with Christ. Jesus isn't trying to take anything from him—He's trying to give him something infinitely better.

This is the beauty of discipleship. Jesus never asks us to let go of something without offering us something far greater in return: Himself. To follow Jesus is to find the pearl of great price, the treasure hidden in a field, the one thing worth giving up everything else to obtain (Matthew 13:44-46). The tragedy of the rich young ruler is that he couldn't see the worth of what Jesus was offering. He saw the cost but missed the reward.

A Question for Us

As the rich young ruler walks away, sorrowful and unwilling to part with his wealth, Jesus turns to His disciples and says, "How difficult it will be for those who have wealth to enter the kingdom of God!" (Mark 10:23). His statement stuns the disciples. In their culture, wealth was often viewed as a sign of God's favor. If the rich, who seem to have God's blessing, can't enter the kingdom, who can?

Jesus presses further: "Children, how difficult it is to enter the kingdom of God! It is easier for a camel to go through the eye of a needle than for a rich person to enter the kingdom of God" (Mark 10:24-25). This striking metaphor vividly illustrates the impossibility of earning salvation through wealth or effort. The disciples, perplexed, ask, "Then who can be saved?" (Mark 10:26). This question gets to the heart of the matter: if salvation isn't attainable by human means, where does that leave us?

Jesus responds with the gospel in its purest form: "With man it is impossible, but not with God. For all things are possible with God" (Mark 10:27). Salvation isn't something we achieve; it's something God accomplishes. The rich young ruler walked away because he trusted his wealth more than Jesus. But Jesus invites us to trust Him, knowing that only He can do the impossible.

Why Riches Are Dangerous

Jesus highlights wealth as a barrier to the kingdom due to its power to deceive. Riches tempt us to trust in what we have rather than in God. They offer a false sense of security, convincing us that we are self-sufficient. Instead of depending on God, we depend on our resources, believing they can provide happiness, identity, or control. For the rich young ruler, wealth wasn't just a possession—it was his god, dictating his decisions and owning his heart.

Wealth also distorts our priorities. It lures us into comfort and complacency, numbing us to the deeper realities of the kingdom. Instead of seeking treasure in heaven, we cling to earthly treasure, believing it will satisfy us. Jesus challenges us to let go of these false securities because they blind us to what truly matters: a relationship with Him.

A Radical Redefinition of Blessing
Wealth symbolized divine favor in the disciples' eyes, but Jesus flips this assumption on its head. True blessing, He shows, isn't measured by material abundance but by surrender to God. The rich young ruler had everything the world values, yet he lacked the most important thing. Jesus redefines blessing as a heart that is fully aligned with God's will.

This challenges us to examine our own assumptions. Do we see material success as the ultimate blessing, or do we treasure Christ above all else? Jesus reminds us that real blessing isn't about what we have but about who we know: Him.

The Impossibility of Salvation
The disciples' question— "Then who can be saved?"—is one of the most profound in Scripture. It acknowledges the futility of human effort to achieve salvation. Jesus's answer— "With man it is impossible, but not with God"—shifts the focus entirely to grace. Salvation is not a human accomplishment; it's a divine gift. With man, it's impossible. But with God, all things are possible.

This truth humbles us, stripping away our illusions of self-sufficiency. It also liberates us. Salvation doesn't depend on our performance or resources; it depends on God's power and mercy. It's not something we earn; it's something we receive by faith.

The Call to Radical Trust

Jesus's teaching confronts us with a choice: will we trust in the fleeting security of earthly riches, or will we fully entrust ourselves to God? Wealth is just one example of the idols we cling to, but this principle applies universally. Whatever we trust more than God—whether it's success, relationships, or control—must be surrendered if we are to follow Him fully.

Jesus's invitation is not about loss but gain. He doesn't ask us to let go of idols to leave us empty-handed; He offers us something infinitely greater: Himself. When we trust Him, we exchange temporary securities for eternal joy.

The Beauty of Grace

Ultimately, this story isn't solely about the danger of riches—it's also about the beauty of grace. The rich young ruler walked away because he couldn't let go of his wealth, but Jesus offers us freedom from the idols that enslave us. When we release what we cannot keep, we receive what we can never lose: the treasure of knowing Christ.

Salvation isn't something we achieve; it's a gift from a God who loves us enough to do the impossible. With empty hands and open hearts, we can come to Jesus, trusting He will give us everything we need and more.

A Call to Surrender

The story of the rich young ruler isn't just about wealth; it's about surrender. Jesus doesn't ask for part of our hearts—He asks for all of it. Following Him means letting go of anything we cling to for security, identity, or worth. It's not an easy call, but it's a life-giving one.

Jesus's call is compelling because He doesn't ask us to give up anything without offering us something far greater in return. To the rich young ruler, He promises "treasure in heaven" (Mark 10:21). To the disciples, He says, "There is no one who has left house or brothers or sisters or mother or father or children or lands, for my sake and for the gospel, who will not receive a hundredfold now in this time… and in the age to come eternal life" (Mark 10:29-30). Jesus doesn't just ask for our surrender; He offers us Himself—the greatest treasure of all.

This isn't about losing; it's about gaining. Jesus's invitation is a call to freedom from the things that enslave us. It's an offer to trade fleeting pleasures for eternal joy, temporal security for everlasting peace, and false promises for the unshakable hope found in Him. We don't walk away empty-handed when we let go of our idols. Instead, we walk away with the joy of knowing Christ, the peace of His presence, and the hope of eternal life.

Jesus isn't just better than our idols—He's infinitely better. Following Him leads to the freedom and fulfillment our hearts were made for. It's not merely a decision to give something up; it's the choice to gain everything we were created to experience in Him. It's the realization that surrendering to Jesus is not a sacrifice; it's the ultimate reward.

REFLECTION QUESTIONS

1. **What is the "one thing" in your life that you struggle to surrender to Jesus?** Can you name it? Are you willing to release it into Jesus' hands?

2. **How does this story challenge your understanding of goodness and the idea of earning God's favor?** Are you stuck in a cycle of earning God's favor, or are you willing to be accepted by God through faith in what Christ did for you on the cross and in the resurrection?

3. **In what ways have you seen God's grace make the "impossible" possible in your life or the lives of others?** Do you remember a time when God showed up in a way that was unmistakably Him? Are you overlooking ways in which He's been at work in the "impossible?"

4. **What does it look like for you to treasure Jesus above all else?** Are there other things your heart clings to which keep you from seeing Jesus as the most worthy of treasuring?

5. **How can you encourage others to confront the idols in their lives and find freedom in Christ?** What does it look like to love others honestly and vulnerably when sharing with your friends your own struggles with your own idols?

CHAPTER 6:
THE SCANDALOUS GRACE OF JESUS

A Question Worth Asking

What kind of person does Jesus choose to welcome into His kingdom? The story of Zacchaeus in Luke 19:1–10 answers this question in a way that should surprise, challenge, and comfort us. Jesus doesn't merely tolerate sinners; He seeks them out. He doesn't wait for the "respectable" to clean themselves up; He goes straight to the outcasts, the misfits, and the despised. Zacchaeus was one such person. His story is a vivid picture of grace—scandalous, transformative, and irresistible.

Zacchaeus wasn't just a tax collector; he was the *chief* tax collector, a man reviled by his community for his greed, corruption, and collaboration with the oppressive Roman government. Tax collectors in first-century Israel were hated figures. They didn't just collect taxes for Rome—they exploited their own people, demanding more than what was owed and keeping the extra for themselves. Zacchaeus wasn't simply part of this corrupt system; he was at the top of it. His wealth was built on the suffering of others, and his neighbors likely saw him as the embodiment of everything wrong with the world.

Yet this man—this traitor—is the one Jesus chooses to visit. It's not an accidental encounter; it's intentional. Jesus calls Zacchaeus by name, stepping directly into his life and offering him a kind of love that transforms everything. This is the scandal of grace: it doesn't operate on merit. It pursues the undeserving and loves the unlovable. In Zacchaeus's story, we see what it means to be truly sought, saved, and loved by God.

This encounter pushes us to confront some uncomfortable truths about grace. It's easy to believe that God's love is reserved for those who've cleaned themselves up, people who are respectable and moral. Yet, Zacchaeus's story dismantles that notion. Grace operates in an entirely different economy. It doesn't reward effort or status; it meets us in our brokenness and changes us from the inside out. Grace is undeserved. It's often shocking, reaching those we'd least expect. And, as we'll see in this passage, it has the power to turn a life upside down—and in the process, it challenges our assumptions about who is worthy of God's love.

Zacchaeus's story also invites us to examine our own understanding of grace. Are we willing to believe that God's love reaches even the most despised and rejected? Are we willing to acknowledge that we, too, are in desperate need of this kind of grace? Zacchaeus's encounter with Jesus isn't just about one man's redemption: it's a mirror for us, reflecting the depth of God's mercy and the radical nature of His kingdom.

The Man Everyone Despised

Zacchaeus wasn't just disliked; he was despised. He didn't merely sin in private—his entire way of life was built on exploiting others. As a tax collector, he worked for the hated Roman Empire, not only collecting taxes but also inflating them to line his own pockets. Moreover, Zacchaeus wasn't just any tax collector; he was the chief tax collector in Jericho, a city known for its wealth. His position meant he likely managed a network of tax collectors, ensuring that the system of corruption worked smoothly—and profitably—for him. In the eyes of his people, Zacchaeus wasn't merely a sinner; he was a symbol of betrayal, greed, and everything wrong with their world.

But his wealth came at a cost. While his coffers were full, his relationships were empty. Zacchaeus had traded community for power, belonging for isolation. He was likely shunned by his family, rejected by his neighbors, and viewed as spiritually bankrupt by the religious leaders. Even the Romans who employed him likely saw him as nothing more than a tool for their gain. Zacchaeus may have been rich in possessions, but he was utterly poor in what mattered most—connection, love, and peace.

Yet Luke tells us something surprising: Zacchaeus was "seeking to see who Jesus was" (Luke 19:3). Why would a man like Zacchaeus, who had everything the world could offer, be so desperate to see a traveling rabbi? Perhaps he had heard stories about Jesus—how He welcomed people like him, tax collectors and sinners, without judgment or condemnation. Maybe he'd heard how Jesus called Levi, another tax collector, to be His disciple, or about the parables that painted God as a shepherd who leaves the ninety-nine sheep to find the one that's lost.

Or perhaps Zacchaeus was simply tired. Tired of the wealth that didn't satisfy. Tired of the isolation that came with his choices. Tired of bearing the weight of his reputation and the guilt that came with it. Whatever the reason, something within him stirred—a longing for a life his money couldn't buy, a hope that maybe, just maybe, he wasn't beyond redemption.

Zacchaeus's curiosity about Jesus wasn't just casual; it was desperate. When the crowd blocked his view, he didn't give up. He ran ahead and climbed a sycamore tree to catch a glimpse of Jesus. This was a humiliating act for a man of his stature and wealth. Yet desperation has a way of stripping us of pride. Zacchaeus wasn't just curious; he was searching for something deeper that his wealth and power could never provide. Little did he know, the One he sought had been seeking him all along.

The Obstacles to Grace

Zacchaeus faced significant obstacles in his quest to see Jesus. The first was the crowd. The streets were packed with people eager to catch a glimpse of the famous teacher, and Zacchaeus, being short, couldn't see over them. This wasn't just a logistical problem; it carried a deeper symbolism. The crowd represented the very people who judged and rejected Zacchaeus. To them, he was the *worst* kind of sinner—someone who profited from their suffering. Their disdain for him would have been palpable, a silent but powerful barrier between Zacchaeus and Jesus. It's not hard to imagine the crowd shifting subtly, perhaps even deliberately, to ensure that Zacchaeus couldn't push his way through.

This wall of rejection speaks to a broader reality about grace. How often do others' judgments and attitudes become obstacles for those seeking Jesus? Zacchaeus's experience reminds us that sometimes the greatest barriers to grace are the very people who should be extending it.

The second obstacle was Zacchaeus's own pride. For a man of wealth and status, climbing a tree was a deeply undignified act. It was something children did—not grown men, and certainly not someone as powerful as the chief tax collector of Jericho. Yet Zacchaeus didn't let his pride stop him. He set aside his reputation, ran ahead of the crowd, and climbed a sycamore tree to catch a glimpse of Jesus. This act of desperation reveals something profound about Zacchaeus: he was willing to risk humiliation for the chance to see the One who might change his life.

Zacchaeus's actions challenge us to consider how often we let our pride prevent us from seeking Jesus. How often do we hesitate to take a step of faith because it might make us look foolish or vulnerable? Zacchaeus could have allowed his position, wealth, and dignity to hold him back, but instead, he humbled himself, driven by a longing for something more.

These external and internal obstacles reflect the challenges many face in our journey toward grace. The crowd may not always be literal, but the fear of judgment, rejection, or misunderstanding from others can often keep us from pursuing Jesus. Similarly, our pride, need to maintain appearances, and unwillingness to admit our need for help can become barriers to experiencing His love.

What makes Zacchaeus's story so powerful is his determination. He didn't allow the crowd's judgment or his own pride to stop him. He found a way to position himself where he could see Jesus, no matter how unconventional or undignified it may have been. His determination reminds us of a vital truth: grace often begins with a desperate search, a willingness to admit that we can't fix ourselves. Zacchaeus didn't let obstacles keep him from seeking Jesus, and because of his persistence, he discovered a grace that would transform his life forever.

The Grace That Seeks

What happens next is nothing short of stunning. As Jesus passes by, He looks up, sees Zacchaeus, and says, "Zacchaeus, hurry and come down, for I must stay at your house today" (Luke 19:5). This isn't a casual glance or a fleeting acknowledgment. Jesus doesn't just notice Zacchaeus; He calls him by name. The One who created Zacchaeus, who knows every hidden corner of his heart, speaks directly to him. In a moment that cuts through the crowd's noise, Zacchaeus becomes the focus of Jesus's attention.

And Jesus doesn't wait for Zacchaeus to invite Him in. He invites Himself into Zacchaeus's life. "I must stay at your house today." These words are filled with urgency and purpose. This isn't a polite request; it's a declaration of intent. Jesus essentially says, "This is why I've come to Jericho—not for the crowd, but for you."

This is grace in its purest form. Grace doesn't wait for us to clean ourselves up, get our act together, or make the first move. It seeks us out, meeting us exactly where we are, regardless of how far we've strayed. Zacchaeus climbed the tree hoping to see Jesus, but it turns out Jesus was already looking for him. This is the scandal of grace: it doesn't operate on human logic or merit. It moves toward the broken, the despised, and the outcasts, offering them a love they didn't earn and could never repay.

For Zacchaeus, this moment is nothing short of life-changing. He climbed the tree out of curiosity, just to catch a glimpse of Jesus. But now Jesus is coming to his house. This isn't just a social visit; it's a declaration of acceptance and belonging. In first-century Jewish culture, sharing a meal wasn't merely about eating together; it was a profound expression of fellowship, relationship, and affirmation. By choosing to dine with Zacchaeus, Jesus makes a public statement: Zacchaeus matters to Him.

This act would have been nothing short of scandalous. To the crowd, Zacchaeus was a sinner, unworthy of such an honor. But Jesus's actions reveal a deeper truth about grace—it doesn't shy away from sin or shame. It moves toward it with love and redemption. Jesus doesn't condone Zacchaeus's sins, but neither does He allow them to define him. He sees beyond Zacchaeus's reputation, beyond his wealth and corruption, and calls him into a relationship that will transform his life.

In this single act of seeking out Zacchaeus, Jesus demonstrates the heart of His mission: "The Son of Man came to seek and to save the lost" (Luke 19:10). Zacchaeus wasn't just climbing a tree to see Jesus; he was being sought by the One who never stops pursuing the lost. This is the grace that seeks—one that finds us where we are but refuses to leave us there. It's the kind of grace that redefines us, not by our failures but by the love of the One who calls us by name.

The Crowd's Resistance

Of course, not everyone is thrilled about this turn of events. The crowd grumbles, "He has gone in to be the guest of a man who is a sinner" (Luke 19:7). Their words drip with disdain and incredulity. To them, Zacchaeus embodies corruption, a man who has betrayed his own people and profited from their suffering. That Jesus would choose to associate with such a person is, in their eyes, unthinkable. Their reaction reveals a deep misunderstanding of grace. They assume that Jesus's association with Zacchaeus is an endorsement of his sin, but grace doesn't condone sin—it transforms sinners.

The crowd's judgmental attitude serves as a warning to us. How often do we act as gatekeepers, deciding who is "worthy" of God's love? It's easy to look at others and measure their sins against our own, thinking they are somehow beyond the reach of grace. Like the crowd, we can fall into the trap of believing that God's love is reserved for those who've lived respectable lives, who haven't fallen too far or strayed too much. But Jesus shatters these categories, showing us that no one is beyond the reach of His love.

Grace is never about who deserves it; it's about the unmerited favor of God toward those who know they need it. The crowd's grumbling also exposes their failure to see their own need for grace. While Zacchaeus's sins were public and obvious, the crowd's self-righteousness was equally dangerous, though far more subtle. Both needed grace, but only one recognized it.

This moment challenges us to examine our own hearts. Do we celebrate when God extends grace to those we might consider "undeserving," or do we grumble like the crowd? Zacchaeus's story reminds us that God's love isn't something we earn—it's something He freely gives. That truth should humble us, removing any sense of superiority and filling us with gratitude for the grace that has been extended to us.

The Transformation of Grace

Zacchaeus's encounter with Jesus leaves him transformed. Grace never leaves us unchanged. In response to Jesus's presence and acceptance, Zacchaeus stands up and makes a declaration that astonishes everyone: "Behold, Lord, the half of my goods I give to the poor. And if I have defrauded anyone of anything, I restore it fourfold" (Luke 19:8). This is no small gesture. It's more than an apology or a token act of goodwill. It represents a radical reorientation of his entire life.

For Zacchaeus, who had built his identity on wealth, this declaration is revolutionary. Money had been his god, his source of power and security, the foundation of his life. Now, he freely gives it away in the light of Jesus's grace. His response goes far beyond what the law required. According to Jewish law, restitution for fraud typically required repaying the original amount plus an additional 20 percent (Leviticus 6:5). But Zacchaeus doesn't stop at the minimum; he promises to restore four times the amount, a level of restitution usually reserved for cases of outright theft (Exodus 22:1). On top of that, he gives away half of his wealth to the poor. This isn't just repentance; it's extravagant, joyful generosity.

Zacchaeus's actions demonstrate what true repentance looks like. It's not merely feeling sorrow for sin; it's turning away from it and toward a life aligned with God's kingdom. His transformation is immediate, visible, and costly. It's as if the grace of Jesus has unlocked something within him, freeing him from the greed and selfishness that once defined his life. What he once clung to, he now releases with joy. Grace has changed his priorities, values, and identity.

Jesus affirms this transformation, declaring, "Today salvation has come to this house, since he also is a son of Abraham" (Luke 19:9). This statement is profound. Zacchaeus, who had been an outcast, is now welcomed into the family of God. He is no longer defined by his past—by his corruption, greed, or betrayal. He is now a true son of Abraham, not because of his heritage but because of his faith. Jesus's words make it clear: salvation isn't about who you've been; it's about who you become when grace takes hold of your life.

Zacchaeus's story vividly illustrates what happens when grace collides with a broken life—it restores, renews, and redefines. Grace doesn't just forgive; it transforms. It changes a man who once exploited others into someone who goes above and beyond to make things right. It replaces selfishness with generosity, greed with justice, and isolation with belonging. Zacchaeus, the man everyone despised, becomes an example of what God's kingdom is all about: redemption and restoration.

This transformation also points us to the heart of Jesus's mission. Zacchaeus's story concludes with one of the most powerful statements in the Gospels: "For the Son of Man came to seek and to save the lost" (Luke 19:10). Zacchaeus was lost—not just morally but also relationally, spiritually, and socially. Jesus sought him out, and grace did the rest. Zacchaeus didn't have to earn Jesus's love; he simply responded to it. In doing so, he found a new identity, a new purpose, and a new life.

The transformation of Zacchaeus challenges us to consider how grace is transforming us. Are there areas of our lives where we're still clinging to old idols, afraid to let go? Have we allowed grace to not only forgive us but also to change us? Zacchaeus's story reminds us that grace is not just about what we're saved *from*; it's about what we're saved *to*: a life of freedom, generosity, and joy in the presence of Jesus.

The Mission of Grace

Jesus concludes His encounter with Zacchaeus with a statement that encapsulates the heart of His ministry: "The Son of Man came to seek and to save the lost" (Luke 19:10). This isn't just a closing comment; it's a declaration of purpose, a mission statement that reveals the depth of God's love and the scope of His redemptive work. In one sentence, Jesus dismantles any notion that salvation is reserved for the morally upright or the religious elite. Instead, He makes it clear: He came not for those who think they're righteous, but for those who know they're sinners.

This is the essence of the gospel. Grace doesn't find us because we're good; it finds us because we're lost. And being lost doesn't disqualify us from Jesus's mission—it's the very reason He came. Zacchaeus's story serves as a vivid illustration of this truth. Here is a man who was beyond redemption by all societal standards. He was morally bankrupt, socially ostracized, and spiritually estranged. Yet he was the one Jesus sought out, proving that no one is too far gone to be reached by grace.

The phrase "seek and save" reveals both the active and restorative nature of Jesus's mission. To seek implies intentionality. Jesus doesn't wait for the lost to come to Him; He goes to them. His pursuit of Zacchaeus is a perfect example. Jesus knew Zacchaeus's name before they ever met, looked for him in the crowd, and invited Himself into Zacchaeus's life. This is grace in action—deliberate, persistent, and personal.

To save, on the other hand, speaks to the result of that seeking. Salvation isn't just about forgiveness; it's about restoration. When Jesus saves, He doesn't merely remove the penalty of sin; He restores our relationship with God, reclaims our identity, and redirects our lives toward His purposes. Zacchaeus's transformation—from a greedy, self-serving tax collector to a generous, justice-seeking follower of Jesus—is a testament to the comprehensive nature of salvation.

Jesus's statement also challenges us to adopt His perspective. Too often, we view the "lost" with judgment or indifference, writing them off as beyond hope. But Jesus sees them with compassion and urgency. His mission was—and is—to seek and save those who are far from God, regardless of how lost they may seem. This includes the morally corrupt, like Zacchaeus, and the self-righteous, like the grumbling crowd. Grace is available to all who recognize their need for it.

Finally, this statement compels us to reflect on our role in Jesus's mission. If the Son of Man came to seek and save the lost, what does that mean for His followers? Are we willing to seek out those on the margins, those the world deems unworthy, and extend to them the same grace we've received? Jesus's mission didn't end with Zacchaeus; it continues through us. His call to seek and save the lost invites us to join Him in the work of redemption, sharing the good news of grace with a world desperate for hope.

Zacchaeus's story reminds us that no one is beyond the reach of grace. Jesus seeks us out, not because we deserve it, but because He loves us. The question is, will we respond like Zacchaeus, letting go of what holds us back and embracing the life-changing grace of Jesus?

REFLECTION QUESTIONS

1. What obstacles—whether external or internal—are keeping you from seeing Jesus clearly?

2. How does Zacchaeus's story challenge your understanding of who is "worthy" of God's grace?

3. In what ways might you be acting as a gatekeeper, keeping others from experiencing Jesus's grace?

4. What would it look like for you to respond to Jesus with the same radical generosity and repentance as Zacchaeus?

5. How does Jesus's willingness to seek out and save the lost give you hope for yourself and others?

CHAPTER 7:
THE THIRST ONLY JESUS CAN QUENCH

What Are You Thirsting For?

What is it you're truly thirsty for? Is it acceptance, success, security, or love? Perhaps it's a sense of purpose or peace, the assurance that your life matters and that you are seen and valued. We all have a well we keep returning to, hoping to draw enough to satisfy the ache in our souls. These wells take many forms: relationships, career achievements, material possessions, or even religious performance. Yet, time and again, they leave us thirsty, longing for something they can never provide.

In John 4, we meet a woman whose life had been shaped by this kind of longing. She went to the well that day seeking water but found something far greater: the living water that only Jesus can give. Her story reveals what happens when our deepest thirsts collide with the grace of God. This encounter isn't just about her; it's about all of us who have ever felt the ache of unfulfilled desires and the exhaustion of searching for satisfaction in the wrong places.

This is one of the most remarkable encounters in the Gospels. Jesus meets a Samaritan woman, a social outcast, and transforms an ordinary moment into an extraordinary opportunity for grace. Her life, riddled with brokenness and shaped by shame, becomes a canvas on which Jesus paints a picture of redemption and renewal. He doesn't avoid her because of her reputation or circumstances; He steps into her story, offering her a kind of love and acceptance she has never known.

Her story is an invitation to all of us who are thirsty to come and drink from the well that never runs dry. It's a reminder that Jesus doesn't shy away from the messiness of our lives; He enters into it, meets us in our need, and offers us something infinitely better than what we've been chasing. Whatever you're thirsting for, this encounter promises that Jesus is the only One who can truly satisfy. The question is, are we willing to leave our wells behind and trust Him to quench the thirst of our souls?

A Meeting That Wasn't an Accident

John tells us that Jesus "had to pass through Samaria" (John 4:4). Geographically, this wasn't accurate—most Jews would have avoided Samaria altogether, taking the longer route across the Jordan River to bypass the region they despised. Centuries of animosity between Jews and Samaritans ran deep, fueled by differences in worship, culture, and ethnicity. Yet Jesus wasn't following geography; He was following the will of His Father. He had to pass through Samaria because He had an appointment with a woman who didn't even know she needed Him.

This wasn't a random encounter. It was a divine setup, planned from the foundation of the world. Jesus, fully aware of what was about to happen, arrives at Jacob's well, weary from His journey. He sits down at the sixth hour—noon, the hottest part of the day. This detail isn't incidental; it's a clue to the woman's story. Most people would draw water in the cool of the morning or evening, when the well was a hub of social activity. But this woman comes alone, at the most uncomfortable time of day. Why? She's avoiding the stares and whispers of the other women in her village.

Her past, choices, and reputation have made her an outcast. She bears the burden of shame, stemming not only from her actions but also from the unyielding judgment of others. Each trip to the well serves as a reminder of her isolation, her failures, and the life she desperately wishes to escape.

When Jesus asks her for a drink, she's stunned. "How is it that you, a Jew, ask for a drink from me, a woman of Samaria?" (John 4:9). Her response is laced with layers of surprise and skepticism. Jews and Samaritans didn't associate with each other, a divide made even sharper by gender roles. Jewish men didn't casually speak to women in public, let alone to a Samaritan woman with a tarnished reputation.

Yet here is Jesus, breaking every social barrier and reaching across every divide to engage her. His simple request for a drink is more than small talk; it's a profound act of grace. He doesn't view her through the lens of her culture, gender, or past. He sees her as someone made in the image of God, someone worth His time, attention, and love.

This moment shows us something vital about Jesus's mission. He intentionally steps into places others avoid and engages with people others reject. He doesn't shy away from uncomfortable conversations or messy situations. Instead, He moves toward them with purpose, compassion, and grace. For the woman at the well, this encounter begins a transformation she never could have imagined. For us, it's a reminder that Jesus seeks us out, meeting us in our brokenness and offering us a grace that changes everything.

The Gift She Didn't Know She Needed

Jesus gently shifts the conversation from the physical to the spiritual: "If you knew the gift of God, and who it is that is saying to you, 'Give me a drink,' you would have asked Him, and He would have given you living water" (John 4:10). With this statement, Jesus invites the woman to a deeper understanding, but her response reveals her confusion. "Sir, you have nothing to draw water with, and the well is deep" (John 4:11). She's still thinking in terms of physical water, rooted in the practical challenges of drawing from a deep well. But Jesus points to something far greater—something her heart desperately needs but doesn't yet recognize.

"Everyone who drinks of this water will be thirsty again," He explains, "but whoever drinks of the water that I will give him will never be thirsty again. The water that I will give him will become in him a spring of water welling up to eternal life" (John 4:13-14). In these words, Jesus reveals the heart of what He offers: not just a temporary fix, but an eternal solution to the deepest longings of the human soul. The water from Jacob's well, as vital as it is, can only quench physical thirst for a time. However, the living water Jesus offers satisfies completely and continually, becoming a source of life within the one who receives it.

This living water is the essence of what Jesus came to give: a life no longer defined by external circumstances or fleeting satisfaction. It's a life rooted in the eternal, where the deepest thirsts for meaning, belonging, and peace are quenched in Him. For the Samaritan woman—an outcast accustomed to rejection and isolation—this promise must have sounded both extraordinary and bewildering. She's intrigued but hesitant. "Sir, give me this water, so that I will not be thirsty or have to come here to draw water" (John 4:15). Her response shows that while she's interested, she's still focused on the practical implications. She's not yet grasping the spiritual significance of what Jesus is offering.

Jesus's invitation to receive living water speaks to all of us. Like the woman at the well, we often look to external sources to satisfy the internal thirsts of our souls. We turn to relationships, success, material possessions, or achievements, hoping they will fulfill us. But these wells run dry, leaving us thirsty again and again. The living water Jesus offers isn't about meeting surface needs but transforming the heart. It's a gift that satisfies in a way nothing else can because it flows from the very presence of God.

Even in her misunderstanding, the woman's intrigue is a reminder of how grace begins. Jesus meets us where we are—confused, hesitant, and often preoccupied with the temporary. Yet He doesn't rush her toward understanding. Instead, He patiently draws her closer, revealing the depths of what He offers one step at a time. The gift of living water is not just a solution to her spiritual thirst; it's an invitation to know and be known by the One who offers it. This moment marks the turning point in their conversation, where her curiosity opens the door to faith.

When Grace Meets Shame

Jesus gently brings her to the heart of the matter. "Go, call your husband," He says. She replies, "I have no husband." Jesus responds, "You are right in saying, 'I have no husband;' for you have had five husbands, and the one you now have is not your husband" (John 4:16-18). These words could have felt like a dagger, but instead, they become the scalpel of a skilled surgeon. Jesus isn't trying to wound her—He's trying to heal her.

This isn't condemnation; it's compassion. Jesus is exposing her brokenness not to shame her but to free her. He shows her that He knows everything about her—the failed relationships, the broken dreams, and the weight of the shame that brought her to the well alone. Yet, despite all of this, He still offers her living water. He doesn't look away from her pain or pretend it doesn't exist. Instead, He meets her exactly where she is, speaking the truth about her life in a way that both confronts and comforts. This is grace in action: Jesus meets her in her deepest place of need and invites her to something greater.

What's remarkable here is how Jesus handles the very thing she's likely spent years trying to hide. Her past is her greatest source of shame, yet Jesus addresses it directly, showing her that nothing about her life is hidden from Him. He knows her fully, yet loves her completely. This is the kind of love that heals wounds, breaks chains, and restores dignity. Jesus doesn't dismiss her sin, but He does not allow it to define her.

This interaction also speaks to the universal human tendency to seek satisfaction in things that can never truly satisfy. The Samaritan woman sought fulfillment in relationships, moving from one to the next, only to find herself thirsty again and again.

Her story illustrates misplaced hopes of turning to broken cisterns that can hold no water (Jeremiah 2:13). But Jesus says, "What you're looking for in these relationships, you'll only find in Me."

Her story is deeply relatable. We all have things we turn to—people, achievements, possessions, or habits—hoping they'll fill the emptiness inside. But like the woman at the well, we find ourselves thirsty once more, longing for something those things can never provide. Jesus's words to her are His words to us: "Let Me satisfy the thirst that nothing else can quench. Let Me be the living water that transforms your life." In this moment, Jesus isn't just inviting her to leave her past behind—He's offering her a future she never thought possible.

Worship That Transforms
Trying to deflect, the woman shifts the conversation to a theological debate: "Our fathers worshiped on this mountain, but you say that in Jerusalem is the place where people ought to worship" (John 4:20). Her question, on the surface, appears sincere, but it's a diversion tactic—a way to steer the conversation away from the deeply personal truths Jesus has just revealed. Yet Jesus doesn't dismiss her question. He sees through the deflection but uses it to take the conversation deeper, redirecting her focus to the heart of true worship.

"The hour is coming, and is now here, when true worshipers will worship the Father in spirit and truth" (John 4:23). In this statement, Jesus revolutionizes the understanding of worship. Worship isn't about a location; it's about a relationship. It's not confined to a temple in Jerusalem or a mountain in Samaria.

Jesus is saying that true worship transcends physical places and is instead centered on encountering God through the truth of who He is and the transformation of our spirits.

This would have been radical for the Samaritan woman. As someone excluded from both her community and traditional worship practices, she likely carried the weight of spiritual rejection. For her, the question of where worship should occur wasn't just theological—it was deeply personal. Could someone like her, with her past and her status, ever truly worship God? Jesus's response is nothing short of revolutionary. He's telling her that access to God isn't about where you've been or what you've done; it's about who God is and what He offers.

By emphasizing worship "in spirit and truth," Jesus shows that rituals or external qualifications no longer bind worship. It's not about the right place, the right heritage, or even the right performance. True worship is about aligning our hearts with God's truth and opening our spirits to His presence. This kind of worship is deeply relational, not transactional—it's about intimacy with God rather than earning His favor.

For the woman at the well, this is astonishingly good news. She has been pushed to the margins of society and religious life, but Jesus invites her into something far greater: direct, unmediated access to the Father. In this moment, He tears down the barriers that had kept her—and so many others—away from God. Worship is no longer a privilege reserved for the elite or the righteous; it's an invitation extended to anyone willing to come to God in spirit and truth.

This conversation reminds all of us that worship isn't about our past, our pedigree, or our perfection. It's about coming to

God honestly, humbly, and with hearts open to His grace. True worship transforms us because it draws us into the presence of a God who knows us fully and loves us completely. For the Samaritan woman—and for us—this is the ultimate invitation: to leave behind the walls and distractions we've built and encounter the God who seeks worshipers in spirit and truth.

The Messiah Revealed

The woman, overwhelmed by the depth of the interaction, says, "I know that Messiah is coming. When He comes, He will tell us all things" (John 4:25). This statement of hope is mixed with uncertainty, as though she's clinging to a faint glimmer of belief that someone might one day bring clarity and redemption to her fractured life. What happens next is breathtaking: Jesus responds, "I who speak to you am He" (John 4:26).

This marks the first time in the Gospels that Jesus explicitly reveals Himself as the Messiah, choosing to do so with a Samaritan woman who has a scandalous past—a person whom society deems unworthy of attention from the Messiah. Yet Jesus, in His grace, chooses her as the recipient of this monumental revelation.

This moment is a window into the heart of Jesus. He doesn't reveal Himself to the religious elite or the powerful, those who might seem most deserving of such knowledge. Instead, He reveals Himself to the broken, the marginalized, and the outcasts. It's a deliberate choice, showcasing the radical nature of His mission. He's not here for those who think they have it all figured out; He's here for those who know they're lost and need a Savior.

This is the mission of grace: to seek and save those who are lost, no matter how far they've wandered. In choosing this woman for such a profound revelation, Jesus demonstrates that His love and salvation are for everyone, not just the insiders or the "qualified." It's a reminder that God's grace doesn't operate on human terms—it moves toward those the world rejects, offering hope, healing, and the promise of a new identity. For the Samaritan woman and all of us, this moment changes everything.

Leaving the Jar Behind

Transformed by her encounter with Jesus, the woman leaves her water jar—the very reason she came to the well—and runs back to her town. This detail is rich with meaning. The jar, a symbol of her daily needs and her constant reliance on temporary solutions, is no longer her focus. She has found something greater. Her physical thirst fades into the background as her soul overflows with living water.

She proclaims, "Come, see a man who told me all that I ever did. Can this be the Christ?" (John 4:29). The same woman who once avoided her community now seeks them out. Her story, once a source of shame, becomes the testimony that leads many in her town to faith. Her words are simple but powerful, pointing not to her own transformation but to the One who made it possible. She doesn't have all the answers, but she has met Jesus, and that's enough.

Her abandonment of the jar is deeply symbolic. She no longer needs the temporary satisfaction of the well because she has found the living water that satisfies her soul. What she had been searching for in relationships and avoiding in isolation, she now finds in Jesus—a love that knows her fully and redeems her completely. Her transformation isn't just internal; it's immediate and visible.

The town that once judged her now listens to her. Her testimony holds weight, not because of her status but because of the authenticity of her experience. They see the change in her and are compelled to find out what—or rather, *who*—caused it. Her encounter with Jesus turns her from an outcast into an evangelist, showing that when grace takes hold of a life, it redefines everything. The same grace that restored her dignity now propels her into boldness, sharing the good news with those who had once shunned her.

This moment reminds us that true transformation doesn't just change us—it compels us to share what we've received. Like the woman at the well, we're called to leave behind our "jars"— the temporary things we once relied on—and run to tell others about the One who truly satisfies. Her story becomes a powerful testament to the ripple effect of grace: when we encounter Jesus, the impact doesn't end with us; it flows outward, drawing others to the living water we've found.

Living Water for All

This story isn't just about a woman at a well—it's about all of us. Like her, we all have thirsts we're trying to quench in the wrong places. We chase relationships, success, possessions, or achievements, hoping they'll fill the void, only to find ourselves coming back empty, thirsty again. And like her, we all carry shame and brokenness that we try to hide, constructing walls to protect ourselves from the judgment of others and even from God. Yet,

Jesus meets us in those very places, not with condemnation but with compassion. He offers us the living water that truly satisfies, the grace that quenches the deepest thirst of our souls.

The beauty of this story lies in its invitation. Jesus didn't come for the self-sufficient or those who believe they have it all together. He came for the weary, the broken, the outcasts—for those who know they are thirsty. The same living water He offered the Samaritan woman is available to us today. It's a gift we can't earn, only receive. But the question remains: will we drink deeply? Will we set aside our defenses and allow Him to expose the broken places in our hearts so that He can heal them?

This story also calls us to action. The Samaritan woman didn't keep her encounter with Jesus to herself. Transformed by grace, she left her jar behind and ran to her community, boldly proclaiming the good news of the One who knew her completely and loved her anyway. Her testimony became the spark that led many in her town to faith.

Will we, like her, leave behind our jars—the temporary things we once relied on—and run to tell others about the One who offers living water? Jesus's invitation is not just for us but for everyone around us. When we drink deeply from His grace, we're not only satisfied; we're compelled to invite others to the well. This is the ripple effect of living water—it overflows, drawing others to the source of true satisfaction.

Jesus offers the same living water today that He offered to the woman at the well. His grace meets us where we are, but never leaves us there. It transforms us, quenches our deepest thirst, and turns our shame into a story of redemption. Will you come to Him and drink?

REFLECTION QUESTIONS

1. What wells are you turning to for satisfaction that continually leave you thirsty?

2. How does Jesus's offer of living water challenge how you view your deepest needs?

3. In what ways has Jesus transformed your life, and how can you share your story with others?

4. How does this story challenge you to view those who are marginalized or looked down upon in society?

5. Are you willing to meet Jesus at your own "well," bringing your brokenness to Him and trusting Him to satisfy your soul?

CHAPTER 8:
THE RESURRECTION AND THE LIFE

What Happens When Jesus Doesn't Show Up?
What do you do when Jesus doesn't show up when you need Him most? What happens to your faith when you cry out to God and the only response is silence? These are not just abstract questions—they're deeply personal ones. At some point, we all find ourselves in the gap between our prayers and God's answers, asking, *Why didn't You come? What are You doing? Don't You care?*

In John 11, Mary and Martha know this gap all too well. Their brother Lazarus, a close friend of Jesus, is gravely ill. They send word to Him: "Lord, he whom You love is ill" (John 11:3). Notice the subtle yet confident tone of their message. They don't demand or beg. They don't even describe the severity of the illness. They simply state the problem, trusting that Jesus's love for Lazarus will compel Him to act. They've seen His power to heal, know His heart of compassion, and trust His timing. Surely, He will come immediately.

But He doesn't. Jesus remains where He is for two more days, and during that time, Lazarus dies. Let that sink in. The one with the power to stop death in its tracks delays, seemingly without explanation. To Mary and Martha, it must have felt like abandonment. Their cries for help had gone unanswered, and now it was too late—or so it seemed.

Let's not rush past this. Can you imagine the questions swirling in their minds? The heartbreak of watching their brother slip away while clinging to the hope that Jesus would arrive just in time? The growing confusion as the hours dragged on, and He didn't come? The devastation when they realized the worst had happened? And finally, the numbness that often follows profound loss—the quiet resignation that says, *I guess He's not coming.*

This story invites us to wrestle with one of the hardest truths of faith: sometimes, God delays. Those delays can feel crushing, but they are never arbitrary. Jesus says to His disciples, "This illness does not lead to death. It is for the glory of God, so that the Son of God may be glorified through it" (John 11:4). His words don't just point to the end result; they also reveal the purpose behind the delay. There's a bigger story at play, one that Mary and Martha can't yet see. Jesus isn't just going to heal Lazarus; He will reveal something far greater: His power over death itself.

What Mary and Martha couldn't understand in the moment—and what we often struggle to believe in our own lives—is that God's timing is always purposeful. Jesus's delay wasn't neglect; it was love. By waiting, He wasn't ignoring their pain—He was preparing them for a revelation of His glory that would deepen their faith and transform their understanding of who He is. In reality, what seemed like absence was the setup for something far greater.

But here's the astonishing part of this story: when Jesus finally arrives, He doesn't offer a one-size-fits-all response. His interactions with Martha and Mary are profoundly different. To Martha, He gives truth. To Mary, He gives tears. This shows us something remarkable about Jesus: He knows how to uniquely minister to each of us. He sees our hearts, knows what we need, and meets us in ways that are perfectly suited to our individual pain and questions. We'll explore this more in their interactions, but for now, take comfort in this: Jesus doesn't just see your circumstances; He sees *you*. And He meets you right where you are.

Meeting Martha with Truth

When Jesus finally arrives in Bethany, Lazarus has been in the tomb for four days. In Jewish culture, this detail is significant. It was believed that the soul lingered near the body for three days, but all hope of life was gone by the fourth day. This wasn't just death—it was finality. Into this atmosphere of grief and despair, Jesus steps not in haste but with purpose. Every delay and every moment of waiting leads to this divine encounter.

Martha, ever the active one, runs out to meet Him. Her words are raw and honest: "Lord, if You had been here, my brother would not have died" (John 11:21). It's a statement packed with emotion. There's faith—she knows Jesus could have prevented this tragedy. But there's also an undercurrent of disappointment, even grief directed at Jesus: *Why didn't You come? Why didn't You stop this?* This is the tension we all feel in moments of unanswered prayer—the heartbreak of believing He could have changed everything but didn't.

Yet even in her grief, Martha's faith clings to hope. "But even now I know that whatever You ask from God, God will give You" (John 11:22). Her faith is remarkable, not because it's unshaken, but because it persists despite her pain and confusion. She doesn't know what Jesus will do, but she trusts Him enough to believe He can still do something. Her words remind us that faith isn't the absence of doubt or pain; it's choosing to trust God even when the outcome is unclear.

Jesus responds not with an explanation but with a promise: "Your brother will rise again" (John 11:23). His words are deliberate, both comforting and mysterious. Martha, rooted in her understanding of Jewish theology, assumes He's referring to the future resurrection at the end of the age—a belief widely held among Jews of her time. "I know that he will rise again in the resurrection on the last day," she says (John 11:24). It's a response filled with faith but also resignation, as if to say, *Yes, I believe in that future hope, but it doesn't change my pain right now.*

But Jesus has something far more immediate—and far more personal—in mind. "I am the resurrection and the life," He declares. "Whoever believes in Me, though he die, yet shall he live, and everyone who lives and believes in Me shall never die. Do you believe this?" (John 11:25-26).

Let that sink in. Jesus isn't just pointing Martha to a future event; He's pointing her to Himself. He isn't simply offering hope for a distant someday; He's offering Himself as the source of life and resurrection right now. Resurrection isn't just something He does—it's who He is. Life isn't just a gift He gives—it's embodied in Him. He's inviting Martha to shift her focus from what He can do to who He is.

Martha's response is remarkable. "Yes, Lord; I believe that You are the Christ, the Son of God, who is coming into the world" (John 11:27). This is one of the clearest confessions of faith in the Gospels. Even in her pain, even with her unanswered questions, she proclaims who Jesus is. Her faith doesn't depend on her circumstances but on His character.

Martha's interaction with Jesus reminds us that He meets us with what we need most in the moment. For Martha, it's truth—a reminder of who He is and what He can do. In our grief and confusion, Jesus invites us to lift our eyes from our circumstances to see Him as the resurrection and the life. And just like Martha, He asks us, "Do you believe this?" This question is not just for her; it's a question for all of us. Will we trust Him, even when we don't understand? Will we believe that He is life itself, even in the face of death?

Meeting Mary with Tears

After speaking with Martha, Jesus calls for Mary, who approaches Him with a completely different demeanor. Unlike Martha, who engages Jesus in conversation, Mary falls at His feet, overwhelmed by grief, her pain spilling out in unfiltered sorrow. Through her tears, she echoes her sister's words: "Lord, if You had been here, my brother would not have died" (John 11:32). There's no question, no request—just the raw ache of loss and disappointment. Unlike Martha, Mary doesn't need a theological explanation; she needs presence. She needs to know that her pain matters to Jesus.

"When Jesus saw her weeping, and the Jews who had come with her also weeping, He was deeply moved in His spirit and greatly troubled" (John 11:33). These words are loaded with emotion. The original Greek conveys not just sadness but a mix of anger, indignation, and sorrow. Jesus is outraged—not at Mary or her grief but at the destructive power of death itself. He sees the devastation death has caused, the heartache it brings, and He is moved to His very core. This isn't a detached observer offering sympathy; this is the Creator of life standing face-to-face with the enemy of life, and He feels the weight of its impact.

Then comes one of the most profound verses in Scripture: "Jesus wept" (John 11:35). It's the shortest verse in the Bible, yet it reveals a depth of compassion that words could scarcely contain. Why does Jesus weep? He knows He's about to raise Lazarus. He knows the joy that's just moments away. But He doesn't rush past the pain of the present; instead, He enters into it fully, sharing in their sorrow.

This is the heart of a Savior who doesn't just see our pain but feels it alongside us. Jesus weeps because He loves. His tears are not a sign of weakness but of deep, unrelenting compassion. They remind us that God is not distant or detached from our suffering—He is present with us in it. He doesn't offer platitudes or quick fixes; He offers His presence, empathy, and ultimately, power.

For Mary, this moment is as transformative as the theological conversation was for Martha. Jesus meets each sister uniquely, giving them exactly what they need. For Martha, it was the truth to bolster her faith; for Mary, it was tears to validate her grief. This encounter shows us that Jesus knows how to minister to each of us personally, addressing the specific needs of our hearts. Whether we need answers or just someone to sit with us in the pain, He meets us right where we are.

Jesus's tears also reveal a profound truth about God's nature. He isn't indifferent to our suffering; He doesn't brush it aside as insignificant compared to eternity. Instead, He takes it seriously—so seriously that He entered our world to defeat the very forces that cause our pain. When we grieve, we grieve with a God who grieves alongside us. And when we weep, we weep with a Savior who has tasted the bitterness of loss and responds with compassion that moves Him to action.

In this moment, Jesus is preparing to do something extraordinary that will erase the tears of that day. But He doesn't skip the mourning to get to the miracle. He shows us that grief and hope are not mutually exclusive in the kingdom of God. They coexist because even in the darkest moments, we are not alone. We are loved by a Savior who feels our pain, shares our sorrow, and ultimately redeems it all.

Confronting the Tomb

Finally, Jesus approaches the tomb. It's a cave with a stone rolled across the entrance, a stark symbol of death's finality. The air is thick with grief and disbelief as the crowd watches Jesus, waiting to see what He will do. "Take away the stone," He commands (John 11:39). His words cut through the silence, but they are met with hesitation.

Martha, ever practical, voices the obvious concern: "Lord, by this time there will be an odor, for he has been dead four days." Her response highlights the reality of the situation—Lazarus's death is not recent; decomposition has already begun. Her words are filled with both logic and doubt, as if to say, *Are You sure? Isn't it too late?* Martha, who professed her belief in Jesus moments ago as the resurrection and the life, now struggles to fully trust His ability at this moment. Her hesitation reflects the tension we all face: believing in God's power in theory but struggling to trust it in practice.

Jesus gently reminds her, "Did I not tell you that if you believed, you would see the glory of God?" (John 11:40). He doesn't rebuke her doubt; instead, He redirects her focus. His words are a call to faith, an invitation to trust not only in what He can do but also in who He is. With His reminder, the stone is rolled away, and the onlookers brace themselves for what's to come.

Jesus lifts His eyes to heaven and prays aloud: "Father, I thank You that You have heard me. I knew that You always hear me, but I said this on account of the people standing around, that they may believe that You sent me" (John 11:41-42). Even in this moment, Jesus teaches, pointing everyone present toward the Father and emphasizing the purpose of what is about to happen—to reveal God's glory and strengthen their belief.

Then, in a loud voice, He calls, "Lazarus, come out!" (John 11:43). Imagine the tension in that moment. The crowd holds its breath, straining to see the impossible. And then, against all logic and expectation, Lazarus emerges from the tomb, still wrapped in burial cloths. The sight must have been both astonishing and terrifying. Jesus commands, "Unbind him, and let him go" (John 11:44), turning the moment of shock into one of release and freedom.

This miracle is more than a display of power—it reveals who Jesus is. By calling Lazarus out of the grave, Jesus demonstrates His authority over death, an authority no one else possesses. But there's an important distinction: Lazarus's resurrection is temporary. He will die again. This moment points to a greater reality, foreshadowing the resurrection Jesus will accomplish through His own death and victory over the grave.

Jesus doesn't just conquer death for Lazarus; He conquers it for all who believe in Him. This miracle is a preview of the ultimate defeat of death, a promise that for those who trust in Jesus, the grave is not the end. Lazarus's story reminds us that Jesus doesn't just offer life—He *is* life. And when He speaks, even the dead must obey.

Faith in the Face of Delay

Why did Jesus delay? It's the question Mary, Martha, and all of us ask in moments of waiting. When our prayers seem unanswered and hope begins to fade, it's natural to wonder if God sees, cares, or acts. But Jesus's delay wasn't neglect—it was love. His timing wasn't a mistake; it was deliberate and purposeful. By waiting, Jesus created the opportunity to reveal a greater glory. He didn't simply intend to heal Lazarus; He planned to demonstrate His authority over death itself, offering a deeper revelation of who He is.

Martha and Mary wanted healing. They wanted their brother to be restored before death took him. Their longing wasn't wrong—it was born out of love and faith in Jesus's healing power. However, what Jesus gave them was something far greater: a glimpse of His divine identity and the ultimate hope of eternal life. His delay wasn't about withholding but about giving them something infinitely better.

This story challenges us to trust Him during the waiting period, even when we don't understand. Waiting doesn't imply Jesus is indifferent to our pain. On the contrary, it often means He is working out a plan that we can't yet see, which goes beyond our immediate needs to accomplish something greater for His glory and our good.

Martha's response to Jesus shows us that faith isn't the absence of questions—it's trusting Him despite them. She wrestled with her disappointment yet still believed in His power. Her faith wasn't perfect, but it was persistent. Mary, on the other hand, reminds us that faith doesn't mean suppressing our emotions. She brings her raw, unfiltered grief to Jesus, and He meets her with tears. Their stories show us that faith and doubt, hope and sorrow, can coexist in the life of a believer.

And then there's Lazarus, whose life reminds us that Jesus can bring life to places we thought were beyond hope. His resurrection points us to the ultimate truth of the gospel: Jesus doesn't just offer life—He *is* life. When we trust Him, even in the face of delay, we can rest assured that His plans are higher, His love is deeper, and His power is greater than we could ever imagine.

Jesus doesn't always act on our timeline, but He is never late. His delays are not denials; they are invitations to see His glory, trust His love, and experience His life-giving power in ways we never imagined. Even in the waiting, He is the resurrection and the life. The question is: Do you believe this?

REFLECTION QUESTIONS

1. How does Jesus's delay challenge how you view His timing in your life?

2. What does Jesus's interaction with Mary and Martha teach you about how He meets us in both truth and tears?

3. Are there areas in your life where Jesus asks you to "roll away the stone" and trust Him to bring resurrection power?

4. How does this story deepen your hope in the promise of eternal life through Jesus?

5. When have you seen God work in unexpected ways through seasons of waiting or disappointment?

CHAPTER 9:
THE WIDOW AND THE SON

When Grief Meets Compassion

Grief is a universal experience. At some point, we all encounter its crushing weight—a phone call in the middle of the night, a diagnosis we weren't expecting, or the loss of someone we love. Grief is indiscriminate; it doesn't spare the young or the old, the wealthy or the poor, the faithful or the doubter. And in those moments, it's not just the pain of loss that wounds us. It's the ripple effects—broken dreams, unanswered prayers, and a haunting sense of isolation. Grief doesn't just hurt; it isolates, convincing us that no one else can truly understand the depth of our sorrow.

Where can we find hope when grief feels like it will consume us? Where do we turn when we feel unseen, uncared for, and unheard? These questions are not new; they've echoed throughout human history in every culture and across every age. The widow from Nain was no stranger to these feelings.

In Luke 7:11-17, we meet a woman whose story is marked by profound tragedy. She has already buried her husband, and now, her only son is gone. In a patriarchal society where men were often the sole providers and protectors, her loss was more than emotional—it was existential. Without her son, she faced a future filled with uncertainty, isolation, and poverty. Her son wasn't just her child; he was her lifeline, her last connection to a world that already seemed unbearably cruel.

Imagine the scene. She's walking in a funeral procession, surrounded by mourners who are weeping and wailing, but none of their tears can match the depth of her grief. Every step toward the burial site takes her deeper into despair. This isn't just the death of a loved one; it's the death of her security, her community, and her hope.

And then, she meets Jesus.

This moment is more than a chance encounter; it's a divine appointment. The story doesn't just show us a miraculous resurrection; it shows us the heart of Jesus. Here is a Savior who sees us in our deepest sorrow, feels our pain as if it were His own, and meets us with life-giving compassion that changes everything. This isn't just about what Jesus does; it's about who He is.

Jesus doesn't just step into the widow's grief—He transforms it. In doing so, He shows us that no matter how deep our sorrow or how hopeless our situation may seem, He is the one who can bring life where there was once only loss. This story reminds us that our grief does not go unnoticed. Our tears are seen, our pain is felt, and our brokenness is met by a Savior who is not distant or detached but deeply present and profoundly compassionate.

This encounter between the widow and Jesus invites us to bring our grief to Him, not because He promises an immediate resolution, but because He offers us something far greater: Himself. In the face of our pain, He assures us that we are not alone, that death does not have the final word, and that His compassion can restore what feels irreparably broken.

Two Crowds Collide

"Soon afterward, He went to a town called Nain, and His disciples and a great crowd went with Him. As He drew near the gate of the town, behold, a man who had died was being carried out, the only son of his mother, and she was a widow, and a considerable crowd from the town was with her" (Luke 7:11-12).

The scene opens with two crowds converging at the gate of Nain, and the contrast between them could not be starker. One crowd is vibrant, full of life and energy, following Jesus and likely still buzzing with awe after witnessing His miraculous healing of the centurion's servant earlier in the chapter. Hope radiates from this group, and their anticipation is palpable as they are drawn to Jesus, eager to see what He will do next.

The other crowd is somber, shrouded in grief. It's a funeral procession, marked by sorrow and loss. At the center of this group is a widow, leading the way as her son's body is carried out of the city. The weight of her loss is almost tangible, her tears speaking of a pain too deep for words. Her situation is dire in a culture that relies heavily on family for survival. She has already buried her husband, and now her only son—her last source of security and connection—is gone. Her future is not just uncertain; it's devastatingly bleak.

These two crowds—one celebrating life and the other mourning death—meet at the gate of Nain. This is not a random encounter. In God's providence, the path of life intersects with the path of death, setting the stage for a moment that will reveal the heart of Jesus and the power of His compassion.

For the widow, this is a moment of unspeakable pain. Her son wasn't just her child; he was her world. He represented her past, present, and future. His death wasn't just a personal loss—it was a societal blow, leaving her without protection or provision in a patriarchal world that offered little support for widows. She was utterly alone, walking a path of grief that no one in her crowd could truly carry for her.

And yet, on this path of despair, she encounters the one person who can truly change everything. As the crowd following Jesus meets the funeral procession, joy and sorrow collide, hope and despair intersect. This meeting isn't just a crossing of paths; it's a divine appointment.

For those in Jesus's crowd, the widow's grief must have felt like an unwelcome interruption. Their excitement about Jesus and His miracles was palpable, and now they were confronted with the harsh reality of death. But Jesus doesn't shy away from the interruption; He steps into it.

This moment reminds us that life is often filled with these collisions—times when joy and grief exist side by side. It's easy to think of life as either good or bad, hopeful, or hopeless, but in reality, it's often a mixture of both. The crowd's encounter with the widow's pain reminds us that Jesus isn't just the Savior of the celebratory moments; He's also the Redeemer in the moments of deepest sorrow.

At the gate of Nain, the scene is set. On one side, life and celebration; on the other, death and despair. But in the middle stands Jesus, ready to show that death doesn't have the final word in Him. What happens next will reveal not only His power but also His profound compassion for the brokenhearted. It's a moment where the paths of humanity and divinity cross, offering hope to all who are willing to see it.

Jesus Sees Her
"When the Lord saw her…" (Luke 7:13a).

This simple yet profound statement reveals the heart of Jesus. He sees the widow—not just her circumstances, but *her*. He doesn't glance past her to the crowd or focus solely on the spectacle of the funeral procession. His attention is fixed on her, a grieving mother whose world has been shattered. In a culture that often overlooked women, especially widows, Jesus stops everything to focus on her.

He doesn't see her as a social outcast, a burden to society, or a problem to solve. He sees her as a person, made in the image of God, worthy of His full attention and love. This moment reminds us that God's gaze isn't impersonal or distant. It's deeply personal and intentional. Jesus's eyes don't just take in her grief; they communicate something profound: *I see you. I know you. I care for you.*

In a world that often turns away from suffering, Jesus leans in. How often do we, in our discomfort or busyness, fail to truly see the pain of those around us? We might glance at someone's hurt but quickly move on, unwilling to enter their pain. Yet Jesus models something radically different. His gaze is one of compassion, not pity. He doesn't view her through the lens of charity but through the lens of dignity. His look says, "You are not alone."

This is the starting point of grace: Jesus sees us in our pain. He doesn't look away, dismiss, or minimize it. His compassion flows not from duty but from the core of who He is. The word used for compassion in this verse suggests a deep, gut-level response. This isn't a detached or polite concern; it's a visceral reaction to the widow's plight.

Jesus's ability to see her also reminds us that God is never blind to our struggles. We might feel unseen in our pain, as if our tears go unnoticed and our cries go unheard. But this story reassures us that God sees it all. He isn't distant or disinterested; He is intimately aware of every detail.

Consider how revolutionary this is. In a society where widows were often marginalized, Jesus steps in and centers His attention on this grieving woman. Her pain matters to Him. And if it matters to Him, so does ours.

When Jesus sees her, it isn't merely an acknowledgment of her physical presence. He sees her whole story—her past losses, her present heartbreak, and her uncertain future. He sees her fears about survival, her isolation from the community, and the depths of her sorrow. His gaze encompasses everything, and His compassion flows from His understanding.

This act of seeing is where redemption begins. Before Jesus speaks a word or performs a miracle, He acknowledges her humanity. His gaze penetrates beyond her circumstances, reaching her very soul. In that moment, the trajectory of her life begins to change.

Jesus's compassionate gaze invites us to ask ourselves: Do we see others the way He does? Are we willing to pause, to look beyond our own agendas, and to truly see the pain around us? And even more personally, do we believe that Jesus sees *us*? That He knows every tear, every fear, and every hidden struggle?

The widow's encounter with Jesus reminds us that the Savior of the world sees each of us as individuals, not as problems to fix, but as people to love. His compassion isn't abstract; it's deeply personal. And in His gaze, we find a love that refuses to leave us in our pain.

Jesus Feels What She Feels

"And when the Lord saw her, He had compassion on her" (Luke 7:13b).

The word "compassion" here carries a depth of meaning that we shouldn't overlook. In the original Greek, it conveys a strong, gut-wrenching response. It's not just sympathy or concern; it's an intense emotional reaction that moves a person to act. This is the kind of compassion Jesus has for the widow. He doesn't merely see her pain—He feels it deeply and personally.

This is not the response of a detached observer or a distant deity. This is the response of God incarnate, who entered into the brokenness of His creation. Jesus doesn't stand apart from her suffering, dispensing comfort from a safe distance. Instead, He steps directly into it, feeling the full weight of her grief as if it were His own.

Think about the significance of this moment. Jesus, who holds the power of life and death in His hands, allows Himself to be moved by her sorrow. He could have performed the miracle without feeling anything. He could have restored her son's life with a simple command and then moved on. But that's not who Jesus is. His compassion is not just a means to an end—it's a reflection of His very nature.

This isn't the only time we see Jesus moved by compassion. Throughout the Gospels, His heart breaks for the suffering of others. He weeps at Lazarus's tomb, even though He knows He's about to raise him from the dead. He feels Mary and Martha's anguish as they grieve their brother. He's moved by the cries of the blind and the leper's touch. Each encounter reveals a Savior who doesn't just acknowledge pain but enters into it.

Why does this matter? Because it shows us that we serve a God who is not indifferent to our struggles. He isn't cold or distant, watching from the sidelines as we endure life's hardships. He is a God who feels deeply, who weeps with those who weep and mourns with those who mourn.

This is a profound comfort. In our moments of deepest sorrow, we often feel alone, as if no one could possibly understand the depth of our pain. But Jesus does. He understands what it's like to grieve, to feel the sting of loss, and to carry the weight of suffering. And because He understands, He draws near to us in those moments, offering not just solutions but His very presence.

Jesus's compassion also challenges us. Do we feel what others feel? Do we allow ourselves to be moved by the pain of those around us, or do we keep our distance, afraid that entering into their suffering will cost us too much? True compassion, the kind Jesus demonstrates, is costly. It requires vulnerability, empathy, and a willingness to step into the messiness of someone else's life.

This gut-wrenching compassion isn't just a passing emotion; it's a call to action. For Jesus, experiencing the widow's sorrow compels Him to intervene in her situation. He doesn't simply offer her words of comfort—He actively addresses her pain. This embodies the heart of the gospel: a God who not only feels but also acts, stepping into our brokenness to bring restoration and life.

In the widow's story, we glimpse the larger story of redemption. Jesus doesn't just feel the pain of one grieving mother; He feels the weight of all human suffering. On the cross, He bore our sins and sorrows, carrying the full burden of our brokenness. His compassion didn't end with His earthly ministry—it extends to us today, meeting us in our pain and offering the hope of His presence and healing.

This moment with the widow of Nain reminds us that Jesus's compassion isn't just an attribute; it's the essence of who He is. Because of this, we can bring our pain to Him, knowing that He doesn't just see it—He feels it, and He is with us in it.

The Impossible Command

"And He said to her, 'Do not weep'" (Luke 7:13b).

At first glance, these words might seem jarring, even insensitive. How could Jesus tell a grieving mother not to cry? Her son is gone, her world has been shattered, and her tears are the natural outpouring of her loss. But Jesus's words are not a dismissal of her pain but a prelude to hope. He's not saying, "Ignore your sorrow." He's saying, "Lift your eyes. Look at Me. Trust Me. I am about to do something that will change everything."

In that moment, Jesus asks for something profound: faith. Faith that He sees her pain, faith that He cares, and faith that

He has the power to act. It's not that her tears are unwarranted; it's that they don't have the final word. Jesus's command, "Do not weep," isn't about suppressing grief—it's about anticipating what He's about to do.

This is the essence of faith: trusting Jesus even when we don't understand. The widow's tears are real, and her loss is devastating. Yet, Jesus is about to reveal a reality that transcends her grief. He invites her, and all of us who read this story, to believe that even in the darkest moments, He is present, powerful, and working.

What's remarkable here is the tenderness behind Jesus's words. He doesn't tell her not to weep because her pain is invalid; He tells her not to weep because her pain is about to be met by His power. This is not a command to move on or minimize her loss. It's an invitation to hope. And that hope is not grounded in abstract optimism but in the person of Jesus Himself.

For us, these words are both a challenge and a comfort. They challenge us to trust Jesus amid our grief, even when the path forward seems unclear. They remind us that faith doesn't eliminate tears but places them in the hands of the One who can turn mourning into joy. And they comfort us with the assurance that Jesus never speaks empty words. When He says, "Do not weep," it's because He is already at work to bring restoration and life.

Jesus's Power Over Death

"Then He came up and touched the bier, and the bearers stood still. And He said, 'Young man, I say to you, arise.' And the dead man sat up and began to speak, and Jesus gave him to his mother" (Luke 7:14-15).

In an extraordinary act, Jesus steps forward and touches the bier, the stretcher carrying the young man's lifeless body. This act alone is astonishing. According to Jewish law, touching anything associated with death would render a person ceremonially unclean, separating them from participation in worship until they underwent a purification process. But Jesus doesn't hesitate. He isn't concerned with ritual purity; He's concerned with the broken heart of the grieving widow.

This touch is more than an act of compassion; it's a declaration of Jesus's authority over death itself. His action says, "Death does not defile Me—I defeat it." Where others would have avoided contact for fear of contamination, Jesus steps in, showing that He is not just immune to death's sting but the One who will conquer it completely.

With a word, Jesus speaks to the young man: "Young man, I say to you, arise." His voice carries the power that spoke creation into existence, the authority that commands winds and waves, and the life-giving force that reverses the finality of death. The young man sits up, alive once more, and begins to speak, serving as proof that he is fully restored.

Imagine the crowd's shock and awe. Their mourning turns to astonishment as they witness the impossible. But for the widow, this moment is far more personal. Her son, who is her only remaining family, her hope and future, is restored to her. Jesus doesn't just perform a miracle; He gives her back what she thought was lost forever.

This isn't just a temporary reprieve from death. While the young man will one day face mortality again, this moment points to a greater reality. It's a glimpse of the kingdom of God, where death will be swallowed up in victory and life will reign eternally. Jesus's power over death here foreshadows His ultimate triumph over the grave through His own resurrection.

For the crowd, this miracle is a revelation of who Jesus is. He isn't just a prophet or a healer; He is the Lord of life. For the widow, it's the restoration of her hope and future. In one moment, her despair turns to joy, her mourning to dancing. And for all who witness it, this act declares that in Jesus, death does not have the final word—life does.

The Response of the Crowd

"Fear seized them all, and they glorified God, saying, 'A great prophet has arisen among us!' and 'God has visited His people!'" (Luke 7:16).

The crowd's response is overwhelming. They are gripped by fear—not a terror that drives them away, but an awe-filled reverence that brings them to their knees. This fear is a natural reaction to witnessing something that defies explanation, something that bears the unmistakable mark of divine power. It's the kind of fear that recognizes, in the presence of Jesus, that they are standing on holy ground.

The miracle they have just witnessed isn't simply an act of kindness; it's a revelation. They don't just see a young man returned to life—they see the One who holds the power of life and death. Their astonishment isn't limited to the miracle itself; it extends to the identity of the One who performed it.

Their words echo the weight of centuries of longing and expectation: "A great prophet has arisen among us!" and "God has visited His people!" These aren't random exclamations.

They are steeped in the history of Israel, a people who have waited for God to intervene, rescue, and restore. The mention of a "great prophet" likely calls to mind figures like Elijah and Elisha, who also performed miracles of raising the dead. The crowd recognizes Jesus as standing in that prophetic tradition, but they do not yet fully grasp that He is far greater than any prophet.

The second declaration, "God has visited His people," carries even deeper significance. For generations, the people of Israel lived with the promises of God's presence, His covenant faithfulness, and His eventual redemption. From the burning bush to the temple, from the wilderness to the exile, they clung to the hope that God would one day come to them in a way that would transform everything. In Jesus, that hope is fulfilled.

The phrase "God has visited His people" is a profound theological statement. It acknowledges that the miracle they just witnessed isn't merely a man's work—it is God's work. They likely mean that God has acted through Jesus in this moment. However, what is unfolding before them is much greater than they realize: Jesus isn't just a prophet sent by God; He is Immanuel, "God with us."

Their response challenges us to consider our own reactions to God's works in our lives. Do we stand in awe of His power and presence? Do we glorify Him for what He has done and what it reveals about who He is? The crowd's reaction serves as a reminder that worship is the proper response to encountering Jesus.

What's striking about this moment is how it bridges the gap between the past and the present. The crowd's declarations tie Jesus to the great acts of God throughout Israel's history while pointing forward to the ultimate act of redemption—His death and resurrection. The miracle at Nain isn't just about one family's restoration; it's a foretaste of the kingdom of God, where all things will be made new.

As the crowd glorifies God, they give voice to the truth that Jesus's actions reveal: God has indeed visited His people. And in Jesus, He doesn't just visit; He stays. He walks among us, heals our wounds, raises our dead, and ultimately gives Himself for our salvation. The awe and praise of the crowd echo through the ages, inviting us to join in their worship and to see Jesus not just as a great prophet but as the living embodiment of God's promise to His people.

What This Story Teaches Us

This story is a vivid reminder that Jesus sees us in our pain, feels our sorrow, and can bring life out of death. It reassures us that no matter how isolated or hopeless we may feel, we are never beyond His compassionate gaze. However, it also challenges us. Are we willing to trust Him in the midst of our grief when the outcome is unclear, and the path forward seems impossible? Are we open to the possibility that His plans, though mysterious and often different from our own, are always good and ultimately for His glory?

The widow of Nain's encounter with Jesus is not just about miraculous resurrection; it's about a love reaching the depths of despair. Her son was restored to life, but more than that, her faith was restored to hope. Jesus didn't simply give her back what she had lost; He assured her of His presence and power.

This story invites us to see that the greatest gift Jesus offers isn't merely the resolution of our problems—it's Himself. In the widow's darkest moment, Jesus steps in, bringing not just life to her son but hope to her heart. His love is the one thing that can never be taken from us, the anchor that holds firm even in the face of life's deepest sorrows.

REFLECTION QUESTIONS

1. How does knowing that Jesus sees you in your pain change how you approach Him in prayer?

2. Are there areas in your life where you've stopped believing Jesus can bring life out of death? What would it look like to trust Him in those areas?

3. How can you show the same compassion Jesus shows to those around you who are hurting?

4. In what ways does this story deepen your understanding of Jesus's power and love? How does it inspire you to trust Him more fully?

CHAPTER 10:
SCANDALOUS GRACE – JESUS AND THE SINFUL WOMAN

Who Deserves Grace?
What if grace isn't what you think it is? What if it's more unsettling, more offensive, and more life-altering than you ever imagined? What if grace shatters your assumptions about others and your illusions about yourself?

In Luke 7:36-50, Jesus is invited to a meal at Simon the Pharisee's home. On the surface, it seems like an honor—after all, Simon is a man of status, a respected religious leader in the community. Inviting Jesus into his home signals recognition of Jesus's growing reputation as a teacher and miracle worker. But the invitation is layered. Simon's intentions are unlikely to be purely hospitable.

Perhaps he is curious about Jesus, intrigued by His teachings, but uncertain about His identity. Maybe Simon wants to assess Jesus up close to determine whether this new rabbi is a prophet or a pretender. Or perhaps Simon's motives are more critical, even skeptical, as Pharisees often view Jesus with suspicion. Simon's actions during the meal suggest a lack of genuine respect. He doesn't extend the customary acts of hospitality—no water for Jesus's feet, no kiss of greeting, no oil for His head. These omissions are glaring for a host, especially one of Simon's standing.

Simon's invitation reflects a tension that often surrounded Jesus. His reputation was polarizing; some saw Him as a prophet, while others viewed Him as a threat. Many were drawn to Him, but not all were willing to submit to what He revealed about their hearts. Simon likely represents this middle ground: intrigued yet unwilling to fully embrace Jesus.

Into this carefully curated setting walks a woman who shatters the social order. Her arrival isn't planned, her presence isn't welcome, and her actions are nothing short of scandalous. In contrast to Simon's restrained skepticism, her love for Jesus is extravagant, excessive, and deeply personal.

This story unfolds not just as a clash between a respectable Pharisee and a sinful woman, but as a confrontation between two opposing understandings of grace. Simon believes grace must be earned, while the woman understands it can only be received. As always, Jesus meets both people exactly where they are, challenging their assumptions and revealing the heart of God.

This isn't just a story about an awkward dinner party; it's a story about us. It invites us to ask hard questions: Who deserves forgiveness? What does real love for Jesus look like? And perhaps most importantly, how do we respond to a grace so radical that it refuses to conform to our expectations?

At the center of this tension, Jesus offers an unsettling and profoundly beautiful response. With a parable and a few piercing words, He turns Simon's world upside down and affirms a woman whose love and faith have been ridiculed by everyone else in the room. This moment forces us to wrestle with our own hearts: Are we more like Simon, guarding our pride and respectability, or more like the woman, willing to bring our brokenness to Jesus in exchange for His forgiveness and love?

This is the scandal of grace: it welcomes the unworthy, offends the self-righteous, and leaves no one unchanged. The question is, will you let it change you?

The Uninvited Guest

"Behold, a woman of the city, who was a sinner, when she learned that He was reclining at table in the Pharisee's house, brought an alabaster flask of ointment and standing behind Him at His feet, weeping, she began to wet His feet with her tears and wiped them with the hair of her head and kissed His feet and anointed them with the ointment" (Luke 7:37-38).

The tension in the room is palpable. This woman isn't just an uninvited guest—she's someone no one would ever invite. Known in the city for her sin, her reputation precedes her. To Simon and his guests, she's the last person who should be near a respected rabbi like Jesus. Her very presence challenges the social and moral boundaries upon which Simon and his peers have built their lives.

Her entrance is as bold as it is desperate. She doesn't come with a prepared defense, a plea for understanding, or even a word of explanation. She comes silently, carrying an alabaster jar of perfume—an item as extravagant as her actions will soon prove.

In a society where her very presence would normally provoke judgment or rejection, she walks straight into the Pharisee's house, past the stares and whispers, and kneels at Jesus's feet.

What gave her the courage to walk into such a hostile space? Imagine what must have been going through her mind as she crossed the threshold of Simon's house. She knew the judgment she would face, the sneers and whispers that would follow her every move. Yet, something about Jesus convinced her that He would see her differently. Perhaps she had heard Him teach about God's mercy, or maybe she had witnessed His compassion toward others who were broken and outcast like her. Whatever she had seen or heard, she believed that Jesus was unlike any other religious figure she had encountered.

She must have seen in Jesus a kindness, authority, and love that gave her hope. She believed that He wouldn't reject her, even though everyone else would. This faith in Jesus's character drove her to take such a bold step. She didn't come to Him expecting condemnation—she came because she believed He would offer her forgiveness and welcome her into His presence.

This is no ordinary act of devotion. It's an unfiltered display of love, gratitude, and repentance. Her actions are both shocking and beautiful, defying the rules of propriety and exposing the depth of her heart.

The alabaster jar alone speaks volumes. In that culture, such perfume was incredibly expensive, often worth a year's wages. This was not an incidental offering; it represented something precious, something treasured, perhaps even a symbol of her livelihood or identity. Pouring it out so lavishly was not just an act of generosity—it was an act of surrender. She was giving her best to Jesus, holding nothing back, declaring with every drop that He was worth everything she had.

But there's more to this moment than material sacrifice. The jar, once broken, cannot be put back together. Its contents, once poured out, cannot be retrieved. This act of anointing is final, irreversible, and deeply personal. It's a profound statement that she isn't just giving Jesus a gift—she's giving Him herself.

Her tears add another layer of meaning. She doesn't merely cry; she weeps uncontrollably, her tears falling on Jesus's feet. This isn't a calculated display but a spontaneous outpouring of emotion, reflecting the deep transformation within her. Wiping His feet with her hair—a profoundly intimate and humble gesture in that culture—only underscores her total vulnerability and devotion.

Her entrance and actions raise an important question: What would drive someone to such boldness? For this woman, it wasn't just desperation; it was the recognition that she had encountered something, someone, greater than her sin. She wasn't there to seek forgiveness but to express her overwhelming gratitude for the forgiveness she had already received.

In this moment, her reputation, the scorn of the onlookers, and even her own past fade into the background. The only thing that matters is Jesus. It's a moment of raw, unfiltered devotion that challenges us to consider how much we're willing to risk and give in response to the grace we've received.

Love Without Restraint

The woman's entrance was bold, but what she did next left the room in stunned silence. She didn't simply linger in the background, hoping to go unnoticed. Instead, she moved closer to Jesus, expressing a love and devotion so extravagant that it defied comprehension. Her actions were raw, unfiltered, and deeply personal—a stark contrast to the cold detachment of Simon's hospitality.

Standing behind Jesus, the woman begins to weep. Her tears fall on His feet, and she wipes them with her hair. She then kisses His feet and anoints them with perfume (Luke 7:38).

For Simon, this is outrageous. For the guests, it's unthinkable. A woman touching a man in this way—especially a woman like her—defies all standards of decency. The act violates every cultural norm and expectation of propriety. But for Jesus, it's an act of pure, unrestrained love.

Her tears are not just an outward display of emotion; they reflect a heart overwhelmed by grace. These aren't tears of guilt or shame but those of gratitude. She understands the depth of her sin and the depth of the forgiveness she has received. Her tears wash the feet of the one who has washed her soul clean.

Then, in profound humility, she wipes His feet with her hair. In that culture, a woman's hair was considered her glory, often kept covered or tied up in public as a sign of modesty and respect. For her to let her hair down, much less use it to wipe someone's feet, was an act of complete vulnerability and devotion. It's as if she is saying, "Nothing I have is too sacred, too personal, or too precious to offer to You."

Kissing His feet and anointing them with perfume deepens the meaning of her actions. These gestures are not just extravagant—they are intimate, personal, and deeply symbolic. Feet were dirty and unclean in that time and place, often the part of the body most neglected. Yet she lavishes her love there, at the very place where others might hesitate even to touch.

The perfume, an item of immense value, represents more than just wealth. It is likely one of her most treasured possessions, possibly tied to her identity or livelihood. Breaking it open and pouring it out is an irreversible act, a symbolic statement that her old life is gone, and her future belongs to Jesus. It creates a vivid picture of the gospel: grace always leads to extravagant love.

For Simon and the other guests, her actions are uncomfortable, even offensive. They can't fathom how someone with such a sinful reputation could act so freely, so publicly, and so intimately toward a respected teacher like Jesus. Their discomfort reveals their misunderstanding of grace. They see her sin as an insurmountable barrier, but Jesus sees it as the very thing that has brought her to Him.

This moment challenges us, too. How often do we approach Jesus with a measured, calculated devotion? How often do we hold back out of fear of judgment, embarrassment, or a desire to remain in control? This woman's love is anything but measured. It's excessive, messy, and unashamed.

No act of devotion feels excessive when we understand how much we've been forgiven. Her actions remind us that love for Jesus isn't about earning His favor—it's about responding to the grace we've already received. True love for Jesus doesn't count the cost; it pours everything out at His feet.

Simon's Silent Judgment

Simon watches this unfold and thinks to himself, "If this man were a prophet, He would have known who and what sort of woman this is who is touching Him, for she is a sinner" (Luke 7:39).

Simon's reaction reveals much about his heart. He sees the woman only through the lens of her sin, defining her entirely by her past. To him, she is nothing more than her reputation, a walking reminder of her moral failure. In Simon's mind, her presence is not just inappropriate—it's offensive. He assumes that her touch contaminates the moment, defiling not only Jesus but also the very atmosphere of his carefully constructed dinner.

But Simon's judgment doesn't stop with the woman; it extends to Jesus Himself. He questions Jesus's credibility, thinking, *"If this man were truly a prophet, He would know better. He would see her for what she is and keep His distance."* In Simon's eyes, Jesus's willingness to let her touch Him proves that He cannot be who He claims to be.

This internal critique exposes Simon's lack of faith. He assumes a true prophet would act as he does—with disdain and rejection toward sinners. Simon has no category for a holy man who would welcome the unholy, nor for a teacher who would embrace the broken. His narrow, legalistic view of God blinds him to the very presence of God sitting at his table.

What Simon fails to recognize is his own desperate need for grace. He is so consumed by the woman's sin that he cannot see his own. He assumes he stands above her, righteous and clean, without realizing that his judgmental heart is just as offensive to God as her outward sins.

This moment confronts us with a hard truth: self-righteousness blinds us to the grace of God. Like Simon, we can become so focused on the sins of others that we fail to see our own. We compare ourselves to those we deem less worthy, feeling justified in our moral superiority. But grace doesn't operate on a sliding scale. It doesn't measure who is "better" or "worse." It confronts us all with the reality that we are equally in need of forgiveness.

Simon's silent judgment serves as a mirror for our hearts. How often do we, like him, view others through the lens of their failures instead of their potential for redemption? How often do we question God's mercy when it's extended to those we believe don't deserve it? And how often does our focus on the faults of others keep us from recognizing the glaring faults within ourselves?

Jesus's response to Simon will reveal the stark difference between a heart that understands grace and one that clings to self-righteousness. But for now, Simon sits in silent condemnation, missing the beauty of what is unfolding right in front of him: the scandalous, transformative grace of God.

A Parable of Forgiveness

Jesus, knowing Simon's thoughts, responds with a parable:

"Two people owed money to a certain moneylender. One owed him five hundred denarii, and the other fifty. Neither of them had the money to pay him back, so he forgave the debts of both. Now which of them will love him more?" (Luke 7:41-42).

Simon answers, "The one, I suppose, for whom he canceled the larger debt" (Luke 7:43).

"You have judged rightly," Jesus says.

This parable is straightforward and direct. Two people owe a debt—one large, one small—but neither can repay it. Both debts are forgiven, and the natural response is that the person who was forgiven more will love more. Simon knows the correct answer, but he doesn't yet recognize the truth Jesus is revealing about him and the woman.

The woman understands her great debt and responds with great love. Her tears, her anointing of Jesus's feet, her entire unrestrained devotion are the actions of someone who knows how much they have been forgiven. She doesn't come to earn forgiveness; she comes because she knows she's already received it. Grace is not a theory for her; it's her new reality.

Simon, however, doesn't see himself as someone in need of grace. He considers his "debt" negligible, if it even exists at all. This self-perception stifles his love for Jesus. He respects Jesus enough to invite Him to dinner but does not see Jesus as his Savior. Simon's failure to recognize his sin blinds him to the depth of God's grace, leaving his love for Jesus cold and calculated.

By telling this parable, Jesus exposes the heart of the issue. The woman's love flows from her recognition of her need for forgiveness, while Simon's indifference flows from his denial of his own sin. The parable compels Simon to confront a painful truth: his lack of love for Jesus isn't because he's better than the woman—it's because he doesn't think he needs Jesus like she does.

This parable isn't just for Simon; it's for us. How often do we underestimate our own need for grace? How often do we focus on the sins of others while excusing our own? The truth is, we're all debtors before God, and none of us can repay what we owe. The only difference is whether we recognize it.

Simon's mistake wasn't in owing "less" than the woman. His mistake was believing his debt didn't matter. Jesus's parable teaches us that the size of the debt isn't the issue—it's the awareness of forgiveness that changes everything. The woman's overwhelming gratitude reflects her understanding of how much she's been forgiven. Simon's lack of love reveals that he doesn't think he needs forgiveness at all.

This moment isn't just about the woman's love or Simon's judgment—it's about us. Are we more like Simon, blind to the size of our debt, or like the woman, fully aware of our need for grace and overwhelmed by it? Jesus's parable invites us to look inward, to measure our love for Him against our understanding of what He has done for us.

Grace isn't about who owes more; it's about recognizing that we all owe more than we could ever repay. When we see ourselves clearly, as debtors forgiven by God, our love for Jesus will naturally overflow. That's the response Jesus is calling for—not calculation, but devotion; not judgment, but gratitude; not pride, but love.

Grace Redefined

Turning toward the woman, Jesus says to Simon, "Do you see this woman? I entered your house; you gave Me no water for My feet, but she has wet My feet with her tears and wiped them with her hair. You gave Me no kiss, but from the time I came in she has not ceased to kiss My feet. You did not anoint My head with oil, but she has anointed My feet with ointment" (Luke 7:44-46).

With these words, Jesus brings the entire encounter into sharp focus. Simon thought he was hosting Jesus, honoring Him by inviting Him to dinner. But Jesus exposes the truth: Simon's invitation was not an act of reverence but one of scrutiny. He was evaluating Jesus, measuring Him against his expectations, and in doing so, Simon completely missed who Jesus was.

Simon's failure wasn't merely a lack of hospitality; it revealed a lack of love. The basic customs of the day—washing a guest's feet, greeting them with a kiss, and anointing them with oil—were not extravagant gestures. They constituted the bare minimum for a host. Yet Simon withheld even these simple courtesies, revealing his indifference to Jesus.

In contrast, the woman's actions are not just extravagant—they are profoundly revealing. She doesn't merely offer water; she offers her tears. She doesn't simply wipe His feet; she uses her hair, a gesture of deep humility and vulnerability. She doesn't anoint His head in a symbolic act of honor; she pours out her most precious possession on His feet, declaring total surrender and devotion.

When Jesus asks Simon, "Do you see this woman?" it's a question that cuts to the heart. Simon had seen her, but only through the lens of her sin. He saw her as a label, not as a person. He saw her as a disruption, not as someone desperate for grace. But Jesus challenges Simon—and us—to truly see her. To see not just her brokenness but her transformation. Not just her past but her potential.

Simon's indifference stands in stark contrast to the woman's unrestrained love. He had kept Jesus at arm's length, offering Him only the semblance of respect. She had drawn near, pouring out her love without hesitation. Simon's self-righteousness blinded him to his need for grace, while the woman's brokenness drove her to the feet of Jesus, where she found forgiveness and love.

Then Jesus says the words that change everything: "Your sins are forgiven" (Luke 7:48).

Her forgiveness isn't earned; it's given freely. Her love doesn't merit her salvation; it's a response to it. She doesn't pour out her tears and perfume in an attempt to win Jesus's favor—she does it because she knows she already has it. Her actions celebrate the grace that has already transformed her life.

This moment redefines grace for everyone in the room. To Simon, grace was reserved for the worthy, a reward for the righteous. To Jesus, grace is entirely different—unearned, undeserved, and utterly transformative. Grace doesn't calculate worth or measure merit; it meets us in our brokenness and restores us.

Grace doesn't wait for us to clean ourselves up or prove our worth. It comes to us when we are at our lowest, when we have nothing to offer, and it gives us everything. This is the gospel: God's love poured out for sinners, not because we deserve it but because He is good.

The Question That Lingers

The story doesn't end with the woman's forgiveness. Luke tells us, "Then those who were at table with Him began to say among themselves, 'Who is this, who even forgives sins?' And He said to the woman, 'Your faith has saved you; go in peace'" (Luke 7:49-50).

The crowd's reaction reveals their inability to grasp the magnitude of what just happened. They aren't debating the woman's forgiveness—they're questioning Jesus's authority. In their minds, only God can forgive sins. For Jesus to declare her forgiven is to claim divine authority. It's a bold, unmistakable statement about His identity.

Their question— "Who is this, who even forgives sins?"—isn't just rhetorical. It's the question at the heart of the Gospels, the one that every encounter with Jesus compels us to answer.

But the story doesn't record their response. It leaves the question hanging, pressing it upon the reader. After all we've seen in this book—Jesus's identity, His compassion, His grace, His power, and His willingness to give Himself for us—the same question confronts us: *Who is this man, and what will we do with Him?*

The woman had answered with her actions. Her tears, perfume, and unrestrained love declared her belief that Jesus was more than a teacher, more than a prophet. He was her Savior. Simon, on the other hand, held back. He couldn't see beyond his self-righteousness or admit his need, and thus he missed the grace offered to him.

And Jesus's final words to the woman echo through the ages: "Your faith has saved you; go in peace" (Luke 7:50). This is the heart of the gospel. It's not our deeds, morality, or religious performance that saves us. It's faith—faith in Jesus, who offers forgiveness freely and completely.

But those words aren't just an ending—they're an invitation. The question that lingers in the air for Simon and the other guests lingers for us too. *What will we do with Jesus?*

Will we, like Simon, cling to our self-righteousness, offering Jesus only a superficial acknowledgment while keeping our hearts at a distance? Or will we, like the woman, come to

Him with our brokenness, gratitude, and love, trusting that His grace is sufficient?

The Scandal of Grace

Like the others in this book, this story shows us the scandalous beauty of grace. It welcomes the outcast, forgives the sinner, and transforms the broken. However, it also confronts the self-righteous, offends the proud, and challenges us to release the things that keep us from Jesus.

Grace isn't comfortable. It doesn't leave us as we are. It calls us to surrender, to devotion, to love without restraint. It asks us to see ourselves clearly—not as people who are "better" or "worse" than others, but as people who equally need forgiveness.

The table at Simon's house may be cleared, but the question remains: *Who is this, who even forgives sins?* And what will we do with Him?

The answer to that question isn't just the conclusion of this story—it's the turning point of every story, including yours. Jesus offers more than a moment of inspiration or a collection of memorable sayings. He offers Himself—His life, His death, His resurrection. He offers the grace that forgives, transforms, and saves.

The question is no longer about Simon, the woman, or the other guests at the table. It's about you. *What will you do with Jesus?* The answer to that question changes everything.

REFLECTION QUESTIONS

1. How does this story challenge your understanding of grace?

2. Are there ways you've acted like Simon, focusing on the sins of others while ignoring your own need for forgiveness?

3. How does the woman's extravagant love inspire you to express your gratitude for Jesus?

4. What does it mean for you to "go in peace," knowing your sins are forgiven?

5. How can this story shape how you extend grace and forgiveness to others?

www.ingramcontent.com/pod-product-compliance
Lightning Source LLC
Chambersburg PA
CBHW070048100426
42734CB00040B/2724